Praise for The *Children*

"The children will lead the way, th   ⌐ ⌐ ⌐ ⌐ ⌐ them! We must be willing to look beyond our fears and conditioned beliefs if we are to align fully with the precious resource that these children are. Dr. Meg shines a beacon of light on a subject that must be understood if we are to survive as a species."

—Bob Frissell, author of *Nothing In This Book Is True, But It's Exactly How Things Are* and *You Are a Spiritual Being Having a Human Experience*

Praise for *The Secret History of Consciousness*

"*The Secret History of Consciousness* is a brilliant reflection of Dr. Meg's personal experience into the dimensional worlds of human consciousness and potential. Only from this source does a book of this nature have any authority in the world."

—Drunvalo Melchizedek, founder of the Flower of Life Workshops, consultant for the Spirit of Ma'at, and author of *The Serpent of Light*

"Meg Blackburn Losey takes us on a fascinating tour of our forgotten wisdom, jumpstarting our memory as she goes. A fascinating read full of riveting information!"

—Penney Pierce, expert intuitive and author of *Frequency: The Power of Personal Vibration* and *The Intuitive Way: The Definitive Guide to Increasing Your Awareness*

"Meg Blackburn Losey is the author of one of my favorite books, *The Children of Now*. In *The Secret History of Consciousness*, her astonishing new book, she examines the mysteries of the past, the puzzles of the present, and most importantly prepares us for what is coming in 2012—yes it's real—with intelligence and humor. Everyone needs to read this book!"

—Glynis McCants, "The Numbers Lady," author of the bestselling *Glynis Has Your Number* and *Love By the Numbers*

Praise for *Parenting the Children of Now*

"*Parenting the Children of Now* is a treasure hunt for your wonder, passion, and authenticity as a person, and also as a parent. Losey presents an upfront and honest approach with a dose of humor, as well as heart wisdom. The easy-to-follow format with discussion, exercises for yourself, and ones to share with your children makes for easy reading and essential practices as you find your get-real self to parent the new generation."

—Dr. Caron Goode, founder of The Academy for Coaching Parents, author of *Raising Intuitive Children* and *Kids Who See Ghosts*

"Don't wait. Read *Parenting the Children of Now* by Meg Blackburn Losey, NOW! This book is required reading for parents raising bright, aware, and sensitive children. Whether you are a teacher, minister, doctor, therapist, or a family member, [you can] benefit enormously from the profound insights, humor, compassion, and practical instructions Dr. Meg offers to help guide us through the magical, yet often challenging, years of growing up aware and, more often than not, invalidated."

—Michael J. Tamura, internationally renowned spiritual teacher, visionary, healer, and award-winning author of *You Are the Answer: Discovering and Fulfilling Your Soul's Purpose*

"*Parenting the Children of Now* encourages outside of the box, honest living in parents that perceptive, intuitive children will feel in their core. It supports parents as they take a close look at their emotional well-being so that they can be fully present and congruent in their parenting. This book will support you in the task of weeding out life's little untruths, making peace with the past, and being intentional in the now. All of this translates into more emotional skill and safety within the family that helps kids feel safe in expressing—and being—all of who they are born to be."

—Catherine Craford, LMFT, ATR, author of *The Highly Intuitive Child*

Praise for *Touching the Light*

"With the emergence of all the vast and new knowledge about energetic medicine, *Touching the Light* is the must-have book for understanding home, health, and healing. It is a must read for anyone everywhere in every aspect of the field of health."

—Dannion Brinkley, *New York Times* bestseller, author of *Saved by the Light* and *Secrets of the Light*

"As a practicing gyn-oncologist, I have observed that western medicine cannot explain the phenomena of placebo effects and spontaneous remissions. It virtually ignores a host of potentially useful therapies such as homeopathy and energy medicine that do not fit its paradigm of cause and effect. With her unique ability to communicate with her non-ascended Masters, Dr. Blackburn-Losey has written the definitive comprehensive text that explains these phenomena at a level of understanding not yet known to the majority of humanity. I highly recommend this book as required reading to all those interested in the evolution of integrative medicine."

—Matthew Burrell, MD

"In her riveting new book, Dr. Meg shares with her readers specific how-tos on developing your skills as a healer. In addition, she shares information about her personal experiences and how she learned to trust that what was happening to her was real. Thank you Dr. Meg for the courage to share your story and teaching the rest of us by your example to 'sit back and enjoy the ride!'"

—Marilu Schmier, author of *Waiting for Weston: A Mother's Story about Raising a Multidimensional Child*

"Merely reading the table of contents for Dr. Meg Blackburn Losey's new book will change your life for the better. Then, if you jump into the rest of her book, I'm sure you'll walk out at the end with a new kind of degree in Divine Sciences. In fact, much of what she offers here will have to become part of our regular education in the coming years if we are to advance as humanity from a body-centric intellectual race into the spirit-centered intuitive one we are destined to be. Hats off, once again, to Dr. Meg for mapping out for us a seldom-charted territory of our spiritual development that we urgently need to understand. Pick up her book and pick a chapter like the one on what it takes to be a good healer, or about your etheric anatomy, or the chapter that addresses what no one wants to talk about, or the one on the healing session, and you'll find that any one of them is worth buying the whole book!"

—Michael J. Tamura, world-renowned spiritual teacher, clairvoyant visionary, pioneer of psychic and healing development, and award-winning author of *You are the Answer: Discovering and Fulfilling Your Soul's Purpose*

"This is a must read for everyone, and especially for those who are looking for alternatives to the confines of conventional medicine and Big Pharma."

—Bob Frissell, Flower of Life facilitator and author of *Nothing In This Book Is True, But It's Exactly How Things Are*

THE CHILDREN OF NOW...
EVOLUTION

THE CHILDREN OF NOW...
EVOLUTION

How We Can Support the
Fast-Forward Evolution of Our
Children and All of Humanity

MEG BLACKBURN LOSEY, PH.D.

WEISERBOOKS
San Francisco, CA / Newburyport, MA

First published in 2014 by Weiser Books, an imprint of
Red Wheel/Weiser, LLC
With offices at:
665 Third Street, Suite 400
San Francisco, CA 94107
www.redwheelweiser.com

ISBN: 978-1-57863-565-8

Library of Congress Cataloging-in-Publication Data available upon
request.

Graphics by Meg Blackburn Losey, Ph.D.
Interior by Frame25 Productions

Printed in the United States of America
EBM
10 9 8 7 6 5 4 3 2 1

In loving memory of Lorrin Danielle Kain
March 1994–December 2009
Dance my little ballerina, dance . . . Finally you are free

and

To Lorrin's mom, Karen Kain
No one can ever know how the loss of a child feels unless they
have been there. What I do know is the fullness of life that you
shared with Lorrin. You are the epitome of motherhood, a shin-
ing example of how to embrace what isn't and make of it what is
possible. My love, admiration, and respect, friends for eternity . . .

Contents

Note to Readers

This book is intended to be an informational guide rather than a means to treat, diagnose, or prescribe. Always consult with a qualified health care professional regarding any medical condition or symptoms. Neither the author nor the publisher accepts any responsibility for your health or how you choose to use the information contained in this book.

Gratitude

It takes a village to create the full story when writing about so many aspects of a greater phenomenon. Sometimes there are those who go above and beyond to assist in keeping facts straight and pushing what might have been a list of dry talking points into becoming multifaceted and more three-dimensional in nature.

To all of the families out there who live this phenomenon every day of your lives, thank you for your courage, your efforts, and your love.

And to the Children of Now, many of whom have written to me and shared your hearts, your fears, I love you back and know that *The Children of Now Evolution* is going to give you another leg to stand on.

Special heartfelt thanks to Dr. Kathleen Pelkey for her assistance in maintaining accuracy in the chapter on vaccines. Kathy's insight and references to information were invaluable.

Immense kudos to my friend Angela Reed, PhD, first for being inspired to get her doctorate in transformative studies and achieving it so that she can be of greater service to these amazing kids, and second but equally, for her deep perceptions and insight on the public school system and its intricate workings.

Many thanks to Nancy Battaglia for her help on the GMO subject. Nancy had a wealth of information and was able to quickly and easily steer me to what I needed.

To Jan Johnson, Michael Kerber, and all of you at Red Wheel/Weiser Books, thank you for believing in me . . . again.

And last but most important, thank you to my husband David for unconditionally accepting me being me. You are a brave man.

When I was five years old, my mother always told me that happiness was the key to life. When I went to school, they asked me what I wanted to be when I grew up. I wrote down "happy." They told me I didn't understand the assignment, and I told them they didn't understand life.
—story attributed to John Lennon

Introduction

In 2006 I released a book called *The Children of Now* with Career Press. Little did I realize the impact this book would have as a paradigm-changing perspective on society. It became a best seller in the United States and abroad. *The Children of Now* is currently available in more than thirty languages across the planet. It has been referred to as a resource for graduate school degrees in education and in other child development fields.

I receive emails and letters literally every day from concerned parents and caregivers, physicians, psychologists, teachers, and others, asking me for advice pertaining to these special children. And children of all backgrounds write me regularly to find out which category they fit in to validate their strange abilities and gifts or sometimes just to say thank you for helping them realize they are not crazy.

I have heard amazing stories about how *The Children of Now* found its way into a person's hands at the perfect time in the perfect place or has literally fallen off of store shelves and hit people on the head. Little children have carried the book to their parents and told them they have to read it. Babies have refused to put it down. Parents have left the book on the desk of their child's teacher or principal. The book just shows up out of nowhere where it is needed, again and again.

As a result of reading *The Children of Now*, a number of adults have set out on a mission to contribute what these spectacular kids need. They have gone back to school, either finishing degrees or embarking on new ones. They have opened schools, camps, conferences, and workshops; written their own books; and put up terrific websites. Grassroots movements have sprung up to support these children. New types of learning environments, Facebook pages, and other media have taken on the role of advocating for changing perceptions and care for our amazingly gifted new generations.

On behalf of the Children of Now, huge thanks for your efforts! Keep up the great work!

Being gifted my entire life, I have gotten comfortable with my intuitive abilities to the point that metaphysical events are often my norm, and when something interesting occurs, I often look to the bizarre first, rather than considering a more common cause. Our intuitive abilities are part of our nature; when we learn how to maintain balance in all parts of ourselves, what is different no longer seems unnatural. After all, there is far more to our world than we can experience with our usual five senses. Sometimes a sixth or even a seventh sense is required in order to reveal the true nature of what is happening. Some things just can't be explained in "normal" terms. Sometimes there is a lot more to what is happening than we even have a frame of reference to see.

This was the case with the Children of Now. When they came to me—telepathically at first—I had no frame of reference to logically assess what was taking place. Instead of tensing up and trying to understand, I have learned to relax and let things unfold, revealing their true nature. It was this relaxed approach that allowed the snowball effect of the Children of Now to take over my life, my reality, my heart.

In the early 2000s I began to hear the voices of children in my head. I kind of felt as if maybe I was losing it. But no, I wasn't crazy—just accessible to a new and really different type of communication. Children who could not speak were reaching out to me the only way they could, wanting to be heard. Oh, I heard them all right. At first I thought my paranormal abilities had taken me right out into never-never land, but as I listened, I realized that the messages were often profound and there was never a command to "have to" or "should" or "must do" anything. In fact some of the messages were really fun, while others were calm, quiet communications of love that filled my very being.

As time went on and I actually met nearly all of my unseen sages in person, I began to learn about a vast happening within humanity. I realized that we are changing in ways we never realized and that those changes will indelibly alter the future of our world. These few brave little souls introduced me to the phenomenon of our new children. I had no idea that I was about to go down a very deep rabbit hole into worlds far beyond those I knew then.

Around that time and even and before I began to hear my amazing new friends, I also worked with families in my alternative healing practice. I had begun to tie strange and disparate pieces together that seemed to indicate recurring symptomatology in many of the kids I worked with. In my mind I had begun to keep track of similarities among the kids who were being brought to me in escalating numbers. It seemed that those who couldn't find medical answers anywhere else had started seeking me out. Parents were often panicky about the insights their kids had as they described angels and spirits or remembered talking to God, choosing their parents, and even who they were in past lives. Many of them had healing abilities and knew just whom and where to touch to make people feel better. Some talked about other worlds, other planets or galaxies, technologies, how to save the planet. The kids had a tendency to bounce all over the place and would appear to be hyperactive or not paying attention. There were other strange aspects too, and it was frightening and frustrating the parents. After all, we are taught that anything out of the norm must be a defect or deficit of some kind. When the Children of Now talk about other realities, in the normal scheme of things it might be time to set up a mental health appointment—but that is just not so with these new kids.

I had no idea at the time where the little beings were taking me or what a wild ride I was about to embark upon; all I knew was that there was a mystery going on. But then again I was no stranger to all things bizarre!

I remember the first time I stood in front of a crowd to talk about the Children of Now. I wasn't feeling confident at all. In fact, it was one of those times in my career when I thought that the audience might just laugh me out the door. Although I do my very best to share my own strange experiences in ways that are humorous and honest, sometimes weird is weird and there is no way to reduce it to anything mundane. So there I was, facing a standing-room-only crowd of people. I started my talk by telling everyone that I had no idea what I was going to say, but whatever it was, we were about to learn together.

Having paid to be there, there were many expectant expressions and admittedly a few skeptical faces in the room until I began to talk about the kids. From the very beginning of my talk, everyone was riveted. No one moved. For over two hours, my audience was captivated. Their questions were heartfelt and sincere, and the breadth of different than normal kids and just how wide the phenomenon was quickly became clear to me.

After our allotted two hours, everyone followed me into the hall, and we continued talking for another hour or more. I realized that weekend what an incredible need there was to share the information I had. I realized that the Children of Now were not only not getting what they needed; they were being hurt by a well-meaning yet archaic society. For a number of years this became my mission. I am still a strong advocate for the children.

Somehow, *The Children of Now* seems to have taken on a life and intention all its own. I have always laughingly said that the kids did that. I don't think I am wrong. They seem to be able to make things happen too.

One morning at eleven, I was scheduled to share a healing session with Weston, my most adept telepathic friend. He was the first child to contact me that way. At exactly eleven, instead of Weston's mom calling me as usual, *Good*

Morning America was on the phone asking me to consult for them about the Children of Now. When I asked how they had found me, they said it was kind of odd; they had just pulled me out of thin air. After agreeing to get them what they needed, I hung up the phone and laughed out loud.

"Weston" I called out, "did you do that?" All I could hear was Weston laughing. Of course he had! He was always quite proud of his doings!

Another day *20/20* called me. The story was similar. They weren't sure what had led them to me, but they just knew that I could help them. Of course I did what I could.

Once I said yes, I would help these kids, it seemed like every time I turned around there was magic and crazy connections happening at every turn.

The excitement about the Children of Now—the subject, the book, the entirety of the phenomenon—thrust me into the public in ways I had never dreamed of. That wasn't what I had been after. For a while the world seemed to have forgotten everything else that I do. I have to admit that was hard. My passion is consciousness and healing along with a serious lust for amateur archaeology and travel to sacred sites. What I realize now is that we were addressing consciousness and healing, just in an entirely different vein than I had previously.

The result of all of this is that my perception of life has changed dramatically. I have realized to the deepest part of my soul what true love and unconditionality are. I have seen these reflected time and again from the children and from their parents and caregivers, each of whom thought that they were alone, isolated from the world, not realizing that there were thousands if not millions of others in the same situation.

As time has gone by, I have personally answered nearly every one of the queries that has come to me. What I have realized above all is that the phenomenon I addressed somewhat tentatively and bravely in *The Children of Now* is much greater than I had imagined. What is happening is not an epidemic; it is a global phenomenon. It is likely happening in your family and to those around you. This spectacular event is ongoing. It crosses all barriers of race, creed, and nationality. It isn't something that we have control over. And it isn't a bad thing.

As you will see when you read this book, we are witnessing and participating in a fast-forward evolution of humanity. Our spirits and our awareness are lifting us into an expansion of reality that previous generations could not have considered. Why? They just weren't capable of doing so.

These days, awareness about our new children has heightened. And now that it has, we are far more likely to take notice of young ones who remember talking to God before they came to earth, kids who are natural-born healers with an astounding command of energy, children who are intuitive and have no regard for what is not true, and another class of kids who have lost touch with reality and begun to live within their own worlds of fantasy, and even others who don't grasp that dead is dead because they are no longer emotionally connected.

I have had the opportunity to talk with, observe, and even teach people all over the world about this phenomenon. In the process I have learned a great deal and have come to understand that there are things happening around the globe that are changing the psychology, behaviors, and belief systems of our children and therefore all of us.

This isn't just an interesting phenomenon; it has many facets, many faces, many names. I truly felt that if I wrote about the kids again, I needed to cover the rest of the story. In this fast-forward evolution of humanity, not only are children affected with amazing insights and gifts, some of them are afflicted with challenges that encompass their bodies, their minds, their beings, and therefore their entire families. Some of them don't seem to be here at all. But are they, yet simply in a capacity we have yet to comprehend?

Besides the Crystalline Children and Star Kids, there are children with autism, Asperger's, as well as children being diagnosed with Asperger's, autism, bipolar disorder, ADD, ADHD, and many other things. Somehow all of these kids and all of their gifts and afflictions seem relevant to this phenomenon, so I have done my best to include them here.

Someday we will look back on this time and know without a doubt that we as a group have done a huge disservice to our children, our families, and ourselves. Sometimes we must extend ourselves into unknown territories and find the answers that are required for a given challenge. One of those times is now. We must foster awareness about all of the changes that are happening to our future generations. We can help them. We shouldn't be hurting them.

In an attempt to cover the entire story I have included chapters to discuss less favorable aspects of our fast-forward evolution. After giving it much thought, I felt that a follow-up book to *The Children of Now* would be lacking if it did not address the deeper, darker things that occur when our children don't get what they need or, in some cases such as vaccines, more than they need. In some ways our world is out of control. Our technology has outgrown our psychology, and when that happens, even though technology is a masterful addition to our daily lives, it has its dark side. Unless we get a grip on the overall situation, we face the possibility of making ourselves extinct because our planet will not have been sustained, and our new exciting conveniences and gadgets will have completely desensitized us to our beautiful individual selves.

There is the spectacularly wonderful part of the phenomenon too. Children who remember their past lives and remember choosing their parents knowing ahead of time what kind of challenges or support those people would bring to them. Kids who are empathic, psychic, advocates for a greater society, and who unabashedly will tell you that their greatest mission in our world is to remind us how to love again, because, as they say, we have forgotten the true meaning of love because we don't remember who we are.

Often the feedback that I got from *The Children of Now* was that parents and caregivers wanted more information, more tools to work with. I have taken these requests deeply to heart. You will find that this book is far less anecdotal and chock-full of information and suggestions.

When I wrote the *Children of Now*, I wasn't the only one along for the ride. There were a number of people mentioned in the book including actual children of the various types, their parents, and their caregivers. Some of those people make an appearance in this book as well. For those who are interested in their progress, there is a complete update on four of my major young friends at the end of the book.

To those of you who have already stepped courageously forward on behalf of the Children of Now, you have all my love and respect. To those of you who are considering doing so or who become lit with passion for these kids, my advice is to have a vision, have a plan. Don't just mean well; know where you are going with it, give it everything that you have, ask for the kind of help you need when you need it, and never look back.

To those parents and caregivers who selflessly attend to these amazing kids every day: Your children are not broken; they are simply differently abled. Love them with all your might, listen to them with all that you are, and know that sometimes it just requires a different set of ears to really hear them. You will find those in your heart.

And to the children, you are pioneers in a wilderness of ignorance and deceit. But that isn't all there is. Look deeper. Don't give up. You came to bring light back into our world. Do not let anything stand in the way of your greater mission. What others say or do is not who you are. Don't hide your gifts. Let them shine. You are not what you do; you are reflections of all that is good, all that is perfect. You are unique, shining aspects of an intricately woven One.

Instead of creating fantasy worlds inside of yourselves, instead of acting out to prove that something is wrong with you, know that you are magnificent beings, reflections of light, who have come to the earth with a great message of love. Stand up and shine with your true nature. Be proud of your differences. Do it with all your might. Shine your truths with the same courage that you have shown to me, and our world will never be the same. This book is for you.

CHAPTER 1

The Children of Now: Who Are They and Why Are They Such a Big Deal?

*Your children are not broken,
they are simply differently abled.*
—Meg Blackburn Losey, PhD

So who are the Children of Now? What do we mean by this term and how do we know if a child is one?

The Children of Now is a term I dedicated to a new generation who have come into our world with different abilities and traits. These amazing souls recognize that our world needs certain changes if we as a people are to survive.

Does that sound crazy? You bet. There are children in our world who remember talking to God in person before they chose to be born. There are children who talk to their parents even before they are conceived or while they are in utero, often stating their names or their purpose for coming into the family or into our world. There are kids who remember who they were and what they did in past lives.

There are children who are empathic, intuitive, and have a great command of energy, healing, love, compassion, and sensitivity far beyond what most of us experience.

Some of these children cannot or will not speak at all but are able to communicate telepathically. Some of these children feel everything everyone around them feels and can't tell the difference between what is theirs and what belongs to someone else. There are kids who command change socially by instigating events in their schools or their environments or children who don't react "normally" to what goes on around them. Some kids have unexplained seizures, fevers, and other medically unexplained issues. Some kids talk about love from the truest of hearts and can see the truth in everything, and some children understand the real motivation behind our actions even when we don't. Some of these kids feel to the deepest parts of their souls, who and what we are beyond the illusions we have set forth in order to feel comfortable, accepted, and safe in our world; they embody truth until we teach them something different. Given their openness to all this input and stimulation beyond our understanding, these are kids who need a framework and guidance if they are to survive at all. Some of them want to just be kids from the perspective of inner greatness that waits to bloom. Others have already brought out forward technologies or become CEOs of their own companies.

Our children have these abilities because they are energetically and therefore harmonically put together differently than previous generations. On the outside they look like everyone else, but other, less visible parts of them shine in new and exciting ways.

Why Is This Happening? Our Energy and the Evolution of Humanity

We are made entirely of energy. How that energy comes together as each of us determines the overall way we function in our known world and even outside of the reality that we know. The entirety of who we are spans many dimensions beyond our three-dimensional world. Our etheric anatomy is a stunningly beautiful array of layers of energy, grid systems, finely tuned subsets, and yes, even other bodies that function in tandem with our earthly bodies.

As we develop, not only do our cells evolve to become different parts of our bodies, our energy system grows complexities that literally hold us together, contribute to our clarity and functioning, and also become our system of harmonics, that is, for lack of better words, our personal symphony. Our individual symphony is unique in all of creation and determines the absolute perfection that is us in the scheme of a much greater reality.

Each of us is a complex field of this energy, which I have explained in depth in my book *Touching the Light*. Within that complexity, we have an external field that is like a huge bubble surrounding us and has several jobs: It literally holds us together. It acts like a translation station between finer frequencies of other less tangible realities and our human nature. It is also our first line of defense.

Have you ever said to someone "back up; you are in my space!"? That person got too close to you and interrupted the flow within your external field by compressing it. When the field became smooshed, it felt uncomfortable. Our external field is very fluid inside and carries information to all parts of the rest of our system. When it is compressed, interrupted, or becomes damaged, our internal communications break down as well. When we don't feel well, our external field may pull in and be smaller for a time to allow the resources contained in it to be optimally used. Later, when we feel better, our fields expand again.

Also in our external field are sets of very fine frequencies. They are spaced exactly evenly through the entire area. The frequency sets rotate and move or, more aptly put, pass along the internal energies and communications in our external field. The fluidity with which our energy flows is affected not only by our feelings and experiences, but also by our environment and those around us. For most of us of previous generations, our field structures tend to be very similar even though our harmonics are unique.

Our external fields adjust, respond, and react in very predictable ways. If we hold in our emotions, our fields may become blocked. If we are traumatized, the flow patterns might change, or the field may even be reshaped. When we have surgery, our external field picks up errors due to the electromagnetic emissions from the machines in the operating room. Those errors cause us to heal more slowly and can affect how we feel every day.

When we are happy, joyful, fulfilled, or excited, our fields expand, becoming larger and even more sensitive, reaching out for more of what is good. When we feel bad or are sick, our external fields become smaller, tighter, thicker, and even change colors and functionality. There are a myriad of changes that can occur in our external fields depending on infinite factors, but up through our generation, those responses and changes have been fairly predictable.

The external fields of the Children of Now are different. Because they have evolved very quickly, the way they look and the way they act and react are unusual, more accurate, and faster. They have a harmonic sensitivity to everything in and around them. It is as if the external fields of our new children have billions of feelers. The children sense everything. They can't help it. The difficulty comes when they experience the feelings of others and don't understand that those feelings aren't theirs and that they are not responsible for how another person feels.

Harmonics

In addition to the external field, each of us is made up of a set of harmonics. Our harmonics are comprised of layers and layers of specific sets each having specific jobs or groups of tasks, such as maintaining the health of our organs. As a whole, our harmonics have everything to do with who we are. There are no two sets of harmonics that are alike in all of creation. If there were, we would cancel each other out.

Our harmonics play a huge role in how sensitive we are to everything. The higher our frequencies, the more sensitive we are. When our harmonics reach a certain level, we become more able to utilize our seventh sense, as I call it, which is our intuitive nature. We are able to tap into what our consciousness is bringing to us 24/7. Our consciousness is aware of everything all of the time. It is not limited to time or space and flits around accessing data from eons. Most of us aren't even aware that this is happening.

The energy fields of our children are evolving at an unheard of rate of speed and development. For them, a normal day likely includes the wisdom of the ages intermingled with everything else they have going in. The Children of Now consider some degree of these abilities as second nature. They think nothing of these abilities because having them is an innate part of who they are. There isn't a separation between their divine and earthly natures. The Children of Now embody both in a balance most of us seek our entire lives.

Our harmonics are comprised of pure energy. Ultimately, when factored down to the very basis of all that we are, energy is the key player. It organizes, reflects its being as reality, and remembers everything it has encountered. In a way, even though we are organized in human form, our energy contains an infinite library of everything that has ever been, is now, and ever will be. That is because past, present, and future are happening all at the same time. In a sense, our universe is an encapsulation of everything that is, was, or might be. All of creation is in a constant state of evolution. Everything is fluid and nothing completely constant. On subtler levels, creation is in a constant state of change. From our dense human form, those changes don't seem so obvious, but they are there.

Generally, the evolution of humanity happens over millennia, but lately there has been a shift. Our world has changed, and our systems must keep up.

On the whole, we are far more intelligent than previous generations. We live in an information age where knowledge and news are passed around the world in real time all of the time. We are exposed to technologies that other ages would consider science fiction. Greater intelligence goes hand in hand with expanded consciousness and conscious awareness.

Before we evolved into the type of human beings we are now, we had very little brain activity outside of our need to survive. Because of that we were in tune with everything in and around us. There was no need to understand; it all just was. Now, our minds are full and extremely active dealing with issues that never mattered in our more primitive stages. As we have evolved, our connection with everything faded, and we forgot how to be so in tune.

We began to be surprised by life events and things that happened in our environments. We began to think our way through our experiences rather than to just act and react. All of that thinking caused our brains to work differently until the time came when we began to see ourselves as isolated from everything else. That sense of isolation came with a whole new set of perspectives including our egos that weigh everything based upon past experiences. We also began to take everything personally.

The brain and the ego developed deceptive practices to assure us of our successes and our safety as well as our self-images. We began to live differently, love differently, and approach life and everything in it from completely changed perspectives from what we had earlier in our evolution.

Balance
Creation has rules and laws that maintain the overall balance in all things. The truth is that humanity has evolved out of our truths and into self-induced illusion. We have become

desensitized. We tend to look outside of ourselves for what we think we need or are missing. We deceive ourselves constantly in the name of feeling safe, accepted, even loved.

But creation demands truth. As the evolutionary process continues, we have begun to shift back to our truer nature. Such changes begin energetically first, then move into the physical plane later.

To embody these changes, our consciousness must realize its lack of limitations. Doing so means going back to an internal balance that is true. To evolve into a state of internal balance means that we will drop certain behaviors and certain other parts of us must wake back up. Our more divine nature, as we call it, is coming forward as a necessity for our survival. As luck (or creation) would have it, we are hardwired to seek our divinity. That information is stored both in our energy system and in our DNA.

All of these factors contribute to a true balance or equilibrium among all the aspects of each of us—our mental, physical, emotional, spiritual, and even higher natures that we don't have names for yet. As all of these parts begin the balancing process, our frequencies change. We start to resonate at much higher frequencies than we ever have. Those higher frequencies vibrate faster and faster, and as a result, the changes wake up parts of us that have long been dormant. As these parts come alive, other parts activate, including our DNA, which is closely linked with our consciousness.

Consciousness is light. It is faster than the speed of light in its abilities to move through and beyond time and space. Our consciousness is, shall we say, online all of the time in such a way that it is aware of everything simultaneously.

The problem is that our brains have not yet caught up. Our thinking nature and our need to know and understand everything in our experiences have blocked our consciousness from coming forward with the unlimited amounts of information it gleans.

Multidimensionality and Changing Consciousness

As a result of the current evolutionary fast-forward, some of the Children of Now experience different abilities with their expanded consciousness. One of those capabilities is being able to see beyond our local world.

Creation is made up of lots of areas called dimensions. We live in one, but there are a myriad of others too. (Remember, everything is made up of organized harmonics.) Depending upon the frequency arrangement, dimensions stack with the heaviest or lowest frequencies at the bottommost position and graduate higher and higher where the finest frequencies and upper dimensions reside. Altogether the array of organized dimensions looks like a giant honeycomb. (*See Figure 1.*)

The dimension that we live in is somewhere on the middle lower end. Our dimension allows for mass and density, or hard-formed reality, objects, and occupants, which we are.

Each dimension contains its own version of reality and sometimes otherworldly beings who inhabit it. Some of those realities—those that are closer to ours—are similar but perhaps on a somewhat different timeline of past or future. Most of us are not aware of other realities because we don't have the capability and awareness to travel

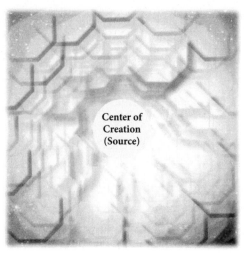

Center of
Creation
(Source)

Figure 1

consciously outside of our own. However, there are some people, especially the Children of Now, who are able to expand their consciousness into other places or dimensions and even interact with those who reside there. Plus, they can learn from the information stored there.

Every part of creation is filled with information stored as light energy. The information constantly changes as everything within creation (including us!) has experiences that alter reality. Think of it this way: When we use our telephone, we are taking advantage of fiber optic lines to convey our voices or perhaps the pure data of our faxes or other communications. We don't really know how it works, but it does. In creation, data is stored similarly, but there are no lines or predictable pathways such as wires. Instead, there is a fluid constant of energy.

In every given moment that constant is different because it is continually responding to the stimuli within it coming from each of us and everything else. The infinite array of energy is in constant motion. As it moves, it also stores information about everything that is happening with, to, and within it. Nothing happens outside of it because there is no outside. Once our consciousness is released from our earthly attention, it can blend and interact in the same form as the living energy that is creation. As it does, consciousness becomes information.

The Children of Now have the natural ability to access knowledge, intelligence, and even wisdom in this way. They can also see and experience living energy so that they may interact with spirits, people who have died but remain close to us. They can go to places and levels of reality that are outside of time and space. That means that they can reach into the past or the future and bring information back to now. Because of this, the Children of Now seem to know a lot more than we think a little kid ought to. Some of these kids seem to carry and expound the wisdom of the ages. This is because their consciousness readily travels and brings home information of all kinds.

What this means is that a child may understand or talk about things that don't fit our reality. He or she may seem to have wisdom beyond words. Energy and information gotten this way is what we call pure in form. It has no boundaries, no navigable path; it just is, and it is everywhere.

Have you ever given someone advice, and then later wondered what the heck you just said or how you knew what you said? During that time, you were so in the zone that you drew information from other planes of reality to help. In a greater, more complex sense, this is what the kids are doing. But just because they can do these things, it doesn't make them weird or mentally ill. What it means is that our children are coming into this world with a seventh sense that operates outside of our current time and space.

When these children come out with statements relative to high science or metaphysical principles or seem to know things that they couldn't have possibly known, they are simply reaching out into the collective energy to get what they need. They are doing energetically what we would use the Internet for. Consider the Internet as an outward example of how creation works. We can use it hardwired or wirelessly. We put information or a word into our search engine and get back a list of information related to our query. Consciousness on the other hand does this much more simply. Consciousness fans out looking for data.

Consciousness grows exponentially. The farther it travels, the wider the spread of energy. Once the fan of energy has collected what it is looking for, it shrinks back down, refining the answers as it does until the concentrated data comes into our brains (or out of our mouths) as knowledge, wisdom, or even a simple answer to something we didn't know.

You might think of this as macro thinking rather than micro thinking, which is entirely linear. A + b = c is linear and a micro way of getting a specific answer. Consciousness uses an array of variables that are literally living light to collect information based upon the questions carried in the array. It not only gives you the answer, it gives a summed-up version of the entire story leading to that answer. Pretty cool, huh?

The Children of Now do this as second nature and aren't even aware of the process. They just seem really wise and intelligent. They are.

New Ways of Thinking and Processing Information

If we are to help the Children of Now, we must first understand how their minds work so that we can recognize that many of the so-called learning disabilities or other seeming defects are merely differences in processing and learn to communicate with them differently.

We have just been discussing how the minds of the Children of Now gather information and refine it. But let's take that a little bit further. Let's look at a hypothetical situation.

Dillon is six years old. He is in first grade, in a typical classroom with another thirty kids. No matter what subject the class is learning, Dillon flits around the room, touches everything, and appears not to be paying attention at all. He is disciplined for his behavior, and it is suggested that he may have attention deficit issues. This goes on every day, and Dillon is often in trouble. Because he is constantly being reprimanded, he begins to lose self-esteem, but he doesn't let anyone know that. Instead, he starts acting out and disrupting the class even further.

No one asks Dillon what he learned on any given day. Instead, he is labeled a problem kid. The real issue is that Dillon is extremely sensitive energetically. Just being in a room full of other kids is hard for him. He moves around in order to shake off the energy buildup that he feels.

In addition, the environment is hard, institutional, cluttered, and his desk uncomfortable. Melanie, who sits next to Dillon, is having a really bad day. Her parents got into a huge fight before she left for school. She is feeling really stressed. Dillon feels her emotions and her confusion at whether or not any of her parents' problems might be her fault, and he can't distinguish that what he is feeling is her issue and not his own.

Dillon's teacher broke up with her boyfriend a few days ago and is sad. Dillon senses that too. Across the room, Billy is really angry. He doesn't like it when he doesn't get his way. He fidgets and causes arguments with the two boys on either side of him. He does this because there are things happening to him at home that he can't talk about. Dillon feels Billy's discomfort as well.

Inside of Dillon all of these different situations and feelings are piling up. He begins to have feelings he can't explain. They aren't his, but he doesn't realize that. The immense dynamics of everything around this little guy are eating at him on the inside. His senses are getting blasted and he is nearly overwhelmed, but no one notices. All everyone sees is a kid who can't sit still.

Had anyone asked him what his experience at school was like today, that person would find out that Dillon's teacher was sad, Billy was really angry, Melanie was having a challenging day, and their science experiments were awesome. He would also describe all the details of his lesson on the Civil War and say that he had to write a paper about his family. He would repeat everything he wrote about. If anyone would just notice, Dillon has a lot to share.

This is a typical honest scenario that happens to millions of kids every day in school, at home, and in social settings.

Why on God's green earth would we punish a child for having a spectacular mind that has the attention to multitask? For our convenience?

The greatest service anyone can give these little sensitives is to teach them how to tell what feelings are theirs and which ones belong to other people. They tend to take it all on as their own. Why wouldn't they if there doesn't seem to be any difference between the feelings on the inside and those on the outside?

A great exercise to do with the Children of Now, especially when they are small, is to talk with them about their day. Ask them how the people around them are feeling or what they observed about them. When one says that when his teacher felt sad he felt sad too, talk with him about that. Ask him if he can tell the difference between his sad and his teacher's. There is a distinction. Once he learns to differentiate feelings, the next lesson is to get him to understand that just because he feels what other people feel doesn't mean that he is responsible in any way for those feelings. A good way to explain this is to use the example of an overheard conversation. It goes like this:

"Okay Dillon, imagine you are in your classroom and you overhear Melanie and Billy talking about their families. When they were talking, you heard them right?"

Dillon would certainly agree.

"But their conversation was between them, right?"

"Right."

"So we could say that you had an observation, but the words were theirs. The conversation was theirs; it was private, right? So even though you know what they said, it wasn't any of your business. Instead, you had an observation. An observation is when you witness something but do not act on it. Not only did your observation not require you do anything, you weren't responsible for what they said or how they felt about it."

"How could I be?"

"Exactly! Feelings are a lot like that. Just because we feel them from other people doesn't mean we made them or they are ours to do something about."

And Dillon begins to get the picture. Teach him how to compare his feelings to an overheard conversation. If he isn't sure, he can ask, "Is this feeling mine or does it belong to someone else?" If it does, then he knows he is having a feeling observation. If the feeling does belong to him, then he can do what is necessary to sort it out. Kids like Dillon carry a lot of guilt for other people's feelings. That is unhealthy and will cause them problems down the road.

Okay, let's go back to Dillon's description of his day when someone finally asked him about it. He had taken in everything around him plus his school lessons, but it didn't seem like he was paying attention at all. Why is that?

The Children of Now process information quite differently than we do. As their consciousness brings in all of these different pieces of information about a multitude of subjects simultaneously, each piece of information is stored compartmentally. Their brains maintain information not categorically, but compartmentally. What this means is that even fragments of information go into relative storage places and become cumulative. One piece of information adds to another and another until there is enough put together for a full story, concept, whatever. Sometimes the pieces all get together to make sense right away, while at other times there may not be enough pieces of information for full logic and so that compartment is on hold until the needed pieces come in.

One can think of this type of mental processing as if the brain has lots of tiny rooms that hold big amounts of information. Each room has a purpose and a subject or task. The doors to the rooms are like saloon doors. They swing both ways. When a piece of information goes in that room, the saloon doors swing back, holding what is inside until the room is full and everything in it makes sense. When it all comes together, the saloon doors swing the other way and let the information out. When that happens, the information comes forward and conscious awareness happens. Until that time, there is no need to dwell on a partial bit of data.

Kids who process in this way are most often labeled or diagnosed as having attention deficit disorder or attention deficit hyperactive disorder. If behavior modification doesn't work (it won't), then the child is likely medicated or isolated from others. He quickly loses his self-confidence or becomes internally angry or depressed. The drugs may make it appear that he is better, but they rob him of his innate gift of being able to lightning-process massive amounts of information. Everyone is happy because now he is more manageable, but he will not learn as much or as deeply and his sense of self has been irrevocably damaged.

In addition to being labeled with behavioral problems, children such as these are often designated as learning disabled. The truth is that we are the ones who are disabled. We don't naturally think like they do. They have information like lightning bolts zipping into specific areas of their brains in seriously rapid time and are simultaneously assimilating the data. The brains of previous generations would short-circuit in a heartbeat if they even tried to work like that.

That our children are being punished, disciplined, medically diagnosed, drugged, altered, in fact downright abused just because their minds work differently is a travesty. We must realize that there is something great happening in the minds of our future generations and then learn how to feed those minds rather than destroy their magnificent natural ways of being.

Awakening to Intuitive Nature

In the evolution of us, the time has come when the brain has reached a state of stasis. Too much input and stimulation, too many demands upon the logical nature of our being. Energetically this can feel a lot like a wet sponge.

Because our brains are working differently just trying to keep up, change is required in order to maintain the stimulation of our growth and our balance both internally and around us. It is only when balance is achieved that we move from surviving to thriving.

Due to all of the input and chaos in our current world, we have barely maintained that intricate balance. On unseen and unconscious levels, we are naturally seeking it.

As many people begin to awaken to their more intuitive nature and to consider the possibilities inherent in worlds beyond ours, they will start to innately remember that there is information in every particle of creation, that healing has much to do with things intangible, and that multidimensionality isn't science fiction. In the coming times, we will begin to see more and more references to consciousness, higher knowledge, things we previously couldn't even realize were possible. We cannot know what is possible until we have an awareness that it may be.

New possibilities are moving into our frame of reference all of the time. Depending upon our harmonic structure, we may or may not even notice. Our brains only pick up less than 10 percent of everything around us. Imagine if we could incorporate that other 90 percent! Kids who seem to be bouncing around oblivious to everything actually are encompassing awareness of a much higher percentage of information.

Where do we think those new possibilities originate? Few people really stop to wonder. The truth is that creation is bringing to us exactly what we need not just to survive but to thrive.

As we evolve into awakening to greater possibilities, we can reach a point of critical mass that will explode among the population. We are there. Not only will our awareness and abilities become more sharply honed to include things that have been outside of our current awareness, we will become contagious simply by our existence.

Our DNA can be affected not only by our environment and what is happening within it, but also by our experiences, our feelings, and how we respond to all of it. As our DNA takes on our perceptions of new possibilities, it alters to accommodate those potential experiences. Then, as more of us teach our DNA these new concepts, our DNA learns so well that the new design becomes hereditary. Then our future generations will have automatically what it took us a long time to learn.

In other words, as we resonate at higher and higher frequencies, those frequencies stimulate different patterns of communication energetically. Those who have not yet awakened begin to because they have been exposed to the higher frequencies of those who are already resonating that way. As they do, their frequencies begin to change, getting higher and higher too.

We have moved through that period and into a place where we are spontaneously changing inside. As we embody our new being and begin to remember what we have forgotten, our next generations are coming into our world with these new abilities already in play.

CHAPTER 2

Categories and Traits of the Children of Now

Our new generations are displaying vast and fast tendencies toward an entirely new structure of human existence. Included in this structure are abilities that we as human beings did not have or were not aware of previously. These gifts are wide and varied, depending on each child. Over time as I worked with countless families and their children, I began to recognize traits that were consistent and predictable in different types of children.

In order to keep it all straight in my head, I came up with a number of names for the categories that suited each type of energy, abilities, and affectedness I witnessed in the kids. Never in a million years did I mean to label the children; I only wanted to be able to communicate about them so that they could get what they needed.

The categories became a world standard as *The Children of Now* book traveled far and wide. Together we have unintentionally set a new norm for the strange and different, and I am, while humbled and in awe of the experience, thrilled that the information I put out there to help the kids has been read and heard.

To best describe the Children of Now, I will continue to stick with these original categories, but I have added a few more to bring things up to date. Most important, all children are special no matter what their abilities or traits. Each child is a gift from the heavens and a contribution to the future of our world. No matter what, they deserve the greatest, most heartfelt upbringing possible!

The Bridge Generation

There is an entire sector of adults in this world who have a deep longing for home. They may or may not have had intuitive gifts early on in their lives, but if they did, they were likely scared of being different and so hid them.

After I released *The Children of Now*, I was inundated with questions by adults who wanted to know how they fit into the overall scheme of the children, for as they read about the children's traits, they recognized themselves. "What category am I?" they all wanted to know.

We are the Bridge Generation. We are the adults who often have a remembrance of home or a sense that we are supposed to return there . . . but where is it? Often we look to the stars seeking an answer, and perhaps are even fascinated with the constellations of Orion, Boötes (the main star of which is Arcturus), or the Pleiades.

We have always known we are different. That sense has plagued us almost from birth. We wonder if we really are natural to the families in which we found ourselves, because we don't seem to fit. We laughingly call ourselves "black sheep," when in fact we really are the one that is lightest!

We have a deep sense of the sacred, but can't say for sure what that is or what it means to us, just that there is a nagging sensation that there is greatness in us far beyond words.

We have had ideas for technologies long before their time, and we have had innate knowings that we don't understand. I remember as a child inventing toothpaste dispensers and cars that had wheels that could turn sideways for parallel parking. We actually have these things now. The August 8, 2013 *New York Daily News* reported: "Electric Car Drives Sideways to Parallel Park."

We are extremely sensitive, even empathic to others. Our sense of intuition has become almost second nature. We know who is on the phone before we answer it or events that will happen in the near future. We have a great pull to find our divine nature and yet for the life of us can't figure out what that is supposed to look like. We try and try and yet don't feel that we ever get there. We have a sense that something huge is going to happen and there is something we must do, but we aren't sure what that is.

For us, normal temperature may be 96.8 instead of 98.6, or run low, as our blood pressure often does too. Occasionally or even often, when we get too excited or mad, we blow the lightbulbs in our homes or elsewhere.

We have perhaps in our lives been plagued with unknown illnesses or medical issues that could not be explained. This may include high fevers that are sustained, temporary paralysis, general chronic fatigue, what is often called fibromyalgia, mild depression, or other unsolved and seemingly unexplainable problems.

We know there is something that we know, but we don't know what it is. We have a sense of a deep truth lying just outside of our grasp, but whatever it is, it is huge. Because of this, we may have sought out alternative religions or belief systems, and we have moved toward the spiritual rather than organized belief systems. We came to realize that spirituality is a state of being, of living, not of believing.

In spite of our different awareness seeming like new territory to us, many of us tentatively or courageously chose to step forward into new and different lifestyles. We chose alternative ways of living, diets, living arrangements, interests, and perceptions. We chose to question standard belief systems. In fact, we began to question everything. And in doing so, we made conscious choices to do things differently. We are changing our world slowly. Our perceptions began to evolve and what used to be considered strange or outside of normal actually became our norm over time.

Intuitiveness, alternative healing, varied belief systems, and alternative life choices are now widely acceptable. More than that, our conscious choices to bring more truth into our lives and the lives of others have become noticeable to the point that there is an undeniable shift taking place.

Many of us have felt insignificant, awkward, alone, different, weird, or worse. We have sought to heal ourselves with every new idea that has hit our path. The truth is that we were never broken. We are just beginning to remember who we have always been. Simply stated, we are who we are, and no matter what that is, it is really wonderful. There is nothing to fix and everything to explore, embrace, and become once we learn to set aside the "shoulds," "musts," and "have tos." There is a beautiful world out there that is filled with rewarding experiences and relationships that have more depth, more light, and greater potential than anything our forefathers could have imagined.

What is important for us to remember is that we are not and never were broken. We are not separate from everyone else. In fact, in many ways we may be the glue that holds us all together. We cannot become victims of our own abilities or perceptions. All we can do is walk in the truth that is us no matter what.

By consciously choosing to become who we are outside of the typical societal standards and belief systems, we have opened the evolutionary door to a greater aspect of human evolution. We made it possible for the Children of Now to enter into a new state of evolution that is clearly recognizable, undeniable, and without a doubt, the fast-forward evolution of humanity. They are coming in droves these days. At first, we noticed just a few differences. Over time, a multitude of changes became apparent.

When you read the traits of some of the children below, you will want to sing out "That's *me*!" Of course it is, but we had to work at it. The kids are getting it all quite naturally!

The Indigo Children

Some of us are able to see energy and its dynamics within the human field. It is a gorgeous, complex array of layers, subtle bodies, power centers, grids, and so much more. The energy moves and flows in predictable patterns, and the colors within the field are astoundingly magnificent as they morph into new or different frequencies. In the 1980s one such person coined the term Indigo Children, because to her the external energy fields of certain kids appeared to be indigo blue. The Indigo Children were the beginning of the phenomenon of the Children of Now. Compared to other categories of the Children of Now, the Indigos seem to have been the briefest. It was as if creation was doing a test run. In that short time a great change overcame the human energy field.

The Indigos are known to have been the paradigm busters. They were able to see the truth in those around them and had no tolerance for untruth. They were not willing to do or be anything just for the convenience of others. This behavior was particularly prevalent in schools; the typical Indigo was no stranger to detentions or other corrective measures!

Indigo Children demanded authenticity. Their intuitive nature wasn't fully developed, but there was something deep inside of the Indigos that insisted on something different from those around them and particularly those in authority over them. They appeared to either be smart alecks as they began to buck the system or not to care. That wasn't it at all. They simply saw the world differently.

The Indigos tended to be laid-back, not greatly motivated toward the hustle and bustle of any structured life, but rather took things as they came, which was maddening to may parents and caregivers. They were very artful—loving music, the arts, nature, anything that flowed with a natural rhythm. Because of their deep-feeling nature, Indigos approached relationships from a very different perspective. They were prone to fewer frivolous peer-type relations in their adolescence and more depth to the ones that did develop.

Many Indigos are currently in their mid to late thirties, but that isn't written in stone. In each wave of the current evolution there are souls who come earlier or later than the average time frames.

The term Indigo has been widely applied in our world as a general reference to all of the Children of Now. Not all kids of the new nature are Indigos though. With the less than subtle differences of the Indigo Children as a launching point, the evolution of our children leaped to great heights once the phenomenon began.

The Crystalline Children

My son appeared in my dreams so often before he was born. It was almost as if we had become friends before he arrived. I knew I was meant to give birth to him at some point. These dreams stopped when I got pregnant.
—Mother of a Crystalline Child

When a Crystalline Child walks into the room, everyone notices. There is something about them. They have charisma, and how it feels to be around them is captivating. They have personalities that are a force and the brains to go with them.

The Crystalline Children began to show up in our world around 1998. The Crystallines are also known by other names such as Rainbow Children, Dolphin Children, and Children of the Sun. The confusion of terms comes from the fact that the energy fields of the Crystalline Children have evolved very quickly in less than a generation.

Early on, the Crystalline Children's energy fields looked like great waves of jewel tone color such as forest green, indigo blue, burgundy red, deep gold, etc. They covered a spectrum of rich color that moved very actively in patterns reminiscent of searchlights in the sky—back and forth, sweeping and absorbing in every nuance around the children until many of them began to get overloaded with input.

Due to the tendencies of their energy patterns, the Crystalline Children innately pick up impressions from everything around them. They latch onto the feelings, motivations, and intentions of others, everything in the visual field, all auditory input, and everything in their tactile range until finally the children become overloaded. Signs and symptoms of this can be noted in odd illnesses or higher body temperatures, even to the point of unexplained seizures. Typically they grow out of these problems as they develop more coping skills.

The Crystallines are so sensitive, that they often can't tell the difference between what is theirs and what feelings, motivations, and intentions belong to others. They begin to carry everything and take the entire world around them very personally. Crystallines can crash from oversensitivity. They must learn to differentiate what is theirs and what is not.

Contrary to popular belief, Crystallines are not blue-eyed sages. The phenomenon crosses all cultural and racial boundaries. A child of any familial background may be born a Crystalline.

If you want something done in an organized and efficient manner, even though they appear to bounce from one idea to another, the Crystalline Children have what it takes. They are great at managing people and giving directions. They can see the logical flow of everything but get disturbed when that flow is interrupted or dysfunctional.

Crystalline Children are extremely sensitive to those around them, knowing how others feel, what they need, what they really mean. They will often reach out intuitively, offering healing hands, a gentle touch filled with heart, and those they touch almost always feel better. They know what to say in even the most difficult situations, and they mean their words from their heart of hearts.

Crystallines often remember where they came from or having a conversation directly with God about coming back to earth and even choosing their parents in the process. They often remember past lives down to minute details of who they were and what they did. Some memories are so specific that the past families or loved ones can be tracked down or at least verified.

Crystallines very often talk to one or both of their parents telepathically even before they are conceived. One of the most common messages they share is their name. They announce themselves. Crystalline Children may also show up in the dreams of their parents when it is easier to reach them. When we are asleep, our everyday defenses are down, and therefore we are easier to communicate with on psychic levels. Crystallines also pop up now and then during their incubation with messages of love or of an intuitive nature.

Crystalline Children are natural-born empaths. Empathic Children of Now innately understand the energy of pain and dysfunction and inherently know how to change that energy to a more positive or well-harmonized nature, making them great healers.

They are enormously love-oriented, heartful, and deeply compassionate. The Crystallines often say that they have come back to the earth to remind us how to love again because we have forgotten who we are and how to connect. They are also extremely socially aware. Often at about ten or eleven, they will set forth something amazing in a very public way.

My granddaughter, a true Crystalline, became angry when her aunt on the other side of the family got sick and ultimately died of pancreatic cancer. It wasn't the cancer my granddaughter was upset about, it was the lack of understanding that we have of the disease. She decided she would raise awareness and funds for research on the subject and single-handedly began making woven bracelets out of yarn and selling them for a dollar. She saved every dollar she made to donate to pancreatic cancer research. Other kids saw the extent of what my granddaughter was doing, and they wanted to participate. Soon she was running a group of forty-two kids in her school library. As word spread of her spectacular efforts, a regional area news network ran a feature story on her. While this sounds like a special case, stories abound of Crystalline Children taking society and its problems by the horns and organizing and acting in the name of change.

You can't lie to a Crystalline Child. They are human lie detectors. They know the truth and will call you on a fib every time. They sincerely want to know the truth and balk when we adults give generic easy answers to avoid getting bogged down in explaining something. My granddaughter used to tell me when she was only four or five that she could see it in my eyes if I wasn't honest with her.

Crystalline Children are peacemakers. They cannot stand conflict of any kind. This attribute is different by far from codependency. It is an honest to God desire for peace in everything. Because of the fine frequency makeup of these kids, if there is too much conflict or no resolution in sight or if there is violence, some Crystallines may actually short-circuit and have seizures.

In addition to this, Crystalline Children are wise beyond their years. They will come up with the most uncanny observations and reflections about the people and situations around them. They recognize the deeper emotions of nearly everyone in their orbit and can accurately speak to those observations if asked.

Crystalline Children are often diagnosed with ADD, ADHD, bipolar disorder, or worse because they can't sit still in the way we were taught and learned to expect of our kids. Crystallines think compartmentally rather than linearly and so can acquire and process massive amounts of data simultaneously. Because of this they are often punished or ostracized for their behaviors. Some are even drugged or worse.

Some Crystalline Children are plagued with night terrors, which are not generally unfounded. They are usually based upon very real experiences. These kids see across the veils and into other worlds. They can see spirits of deceased people who reside just outside of our reality and for some reason or another have not moved on. The frequencies emitted by the Crystalline Children act like a beacon across dimensions attracting spirits and other entities who know the children can see them. With certain harmonic resonance comes innate intuitive ability. When a child or anyone else reaches that resonance or is naturally emitting the frequencies of higher resonance, it is as if they are walking radio stations that can be dialed into from the other side.

Crystalline Children often talk about those they see and even interact with, giving vivid descriptions of their appearances and even their conversations. Because of this they are often misunderstood as having "invisible friends" and told that the visitations are not real.

Unfortunately not all of the visitors are friendly or of good intentions. Usually they have very selfish reasons for contacting the children, such as something they left unsaid or done. Some are quite curious about the children due to their resonance. There are others who visit the children at night simply to observe them.

Crystallines report beings that are very doglike in appearance with lots of wrinkles. They usually come in fours and stand by the bed unspeaking and barely moving. It is as if they are guardians standing at attention. They do nothing and harm no one, but they can be terrifying to a small child. They are apparently extremely intimidating as they stare at the kids in silence.

Other children have reported beings who are golden and are quite commanding in nature. Some descriptions suggest Egyptian or Mayan-type garb. These also come in multiples and seem to only observe. They do no harm, and it is my sense that they are in some ways guardians along the lines of the concept of a guardian angel. Crystallines appear to have an entire troupe.

These types of visitations only seem to occur in the child's bedroom or bathroom. When they happen, the Crystalline Children can display a seemingly unreasonable fear of the bedroom and or bathroom. When the Crystallines see and talk to other spirits, it is not necessarily limited to home. The kids may meet previous inhabitants of their homes or neighborhoods or may be contacted by their own deceased relatives. They may see spirits attached to other places or people. No matter what type of event the kids experience, care should be given to show them support. We should never tell them that their experiences aren't real. They are vividly so.

There is another piece to this whole spirit communication issue. Children may begin to feel responsible for the spirit's situation. What I mean is that the kids can start taking everything personally. When they do, they can get emotionally bogged down or even depressed. Children with these kinds of abilities should be taught to ascertain what is theirs and what belongs to someone else. It is vital that they learn this young so that they don't carry these feelings as their own later on.

The Crystalline Children have become the largest group of our new evolution. My educated estimate is that over 25 percent of children born after 1998 carry Crystalline traits.

The energy fields of the Crystalline Children continue to evolve rapidly. Some who began with deep jewel tones have moved on to pastel colors or even to a unified white field.

The Star Kids

The Star Kids share many of the traits that the Crystalline Children have, particularly the innate ability to heal others and their intuitive nature. Beyond these similarities are traits specific to Stars.

Physically, Star Kids tend to be slim with smaller bodies than other children. Their heads at first seem large and their eyes rounder than most. Sometimes their mouths are small as well.

Star Kids are deeply loving children but also need time alone. They are highly intelligent, introspective, and oriented on the sciences as well as technology. They love to invent things! Give Star Kids a pile of seemingly unrelated things, and they will create wonders with their imagination and deep knowing of how things can work.

While the Crystalline Children are really about people, love, and coming together, the Star Kids are quite concerned for the planet. They seem to feel what is happening within it all of the time. They are terribly worried about the state of the earth and often consider how we can improve how we live on it. For example, the amount of waste products that can be seen at any time in the waterways or along highways upsets these kids to no end. Pollution, drilling and fracking, or anything that disturbs the natural order brings a deep sense of loss or anger to the Star Kids. Somehow in their young wisdom the Star Kids understand the delicate balance between humans and our planet. They can easily recognize when that balance is being threatened.

Star Kids are also extremely in tune with earth activities and may sense earthquakes or large storms prior to them happening. If you were to keep track of earthquake activity, likely you would notice that your child's behavior is directly linked to the rhythm of earth events. For instance, just before an actual earthquake, there is a burst of energy released from deep within the planet. When a child has an energy field that is extremely fine, any disturbance in the continuum can be felt. That being said, the child may react to these felt energy bursts by displaying erratic or disturbed behavior during that time or just preceding an earthquake. Large storms may also affect the Star Kid but not as profoundly as earthquakes will. Some adults have this same sensitivity and will feel nauseous or off balance, or have headaches right around the time of the pre-earthquake energy release.

Star Kids often dream of falling or flying and will describe their experiences in great detail. Their dreamtime directly resembles stories recounted by alien abductees. It is not uncommon for these dreams or experiences to run through the entire family or specific family members. Star Kids are of a particular genome, and their traits, although more refined, are hereditary. Parents of Star Kids often have low basal temperatures around 96.8 and show characteristics of the Bridge Generation in that they deeply long for home, wherever home is.

The energy field of the Star Kids is of such a high frequency they have been known to blank out streetlamps as they walk under them or to blow out electronics such as computers and PDAs.

Star Kids can be adept at telepathic communication and even telekinesis. Their psychic abilities range from pretty good to profound. Star Kids seem to have connections with many worlds.

They easily travel out of their bodies and have an innate awareness of other dimensional realities. They are known for having "friends" from other worlds, invisible to the eyes of adults, but very real. They may receive "downloads"— sudden awareness and knowledge of things they couldn't have possibly gleaned from normal everyday learning. They may also appear to be connected with a certain person or entity outside of our reality who teaches them or brings them knowing regularly or on occasion.

Star Kids can walk outside of time, so that time seemingly slows or stops, or they can accomplish tasks without the clock moving. The Star Kids have a very commanding presence, and when they walk into a room, everyone not only notices, but also waits for what is next. The Star Kids really know how to be heard. They speak with authority and are usually quite correct in their facts.

As they grow older, the Star Kids retain their youthful appearance.

Children of Light

There is a new group of children being born over the past few years who have completely white energy fields. Their energy appears translucent and is at the same time calm almost to a point of stillness and vitally expressive. It is such a subtle field that it may be difficult to comprehend when we have been touched by it.

The energy is white because these fields incorporate every frequency on the spectrum of color, light, and energy. This is the same kind of energy from which we were all made in the dawn of creation and carries messages of our beginning. It is all potential, waiting for an impetus, for instructions, to become something else.

We do not know a whole lot yet about the effect the Children of Light are having on people and our world in general. Time will tell, but what I have seen is that anyone who is touched by the light of one of these babies will be forever changed. It will be as if the breath of God has whispered through one's very being asking us to remember . . .

The Children of Light don't need to do anything but exist to share what they bring. They carry the same frequencies to us that we were created from. These frequencies are the light of our source, the very basis from which all things are made. What types of abilities they may have remains to be seen, but it is an exciting glimpse into the future of humankind.

The Transitional Children

The Transitional Children are also in a class all their own. I first coined this term in 2006 as I observed a group of kids who were a little older than the Crystallines and Stars but had some of the traits without, apparently, the ability to apply or process them. These kids showed up between the Indigo Children and the advent of the Crystallines and are still active today in our communities as they continue to come into our world. This group of kids walks a treacherous line between living life and self-destruction or the destruction of others.

The Transitional Children are extremely sensitive, but instead of talking about their sensitivities or learning how to apply them, they tend to turn inward. By doing so, they unintentionally deceive those around them into believing that everything is fine or that they are simply loners. This is not the case at all. I will be exploring this more in depth in a later chapter, but the Transitional Child is an at risk child and needs great attention due to tendencies toward self-destructive behaviors such as taking drugs, abusing alcohol, self-mutilation, and even suicide or harming others. Generally it is the suicidal tendencies that win out.

Transitional Children develop extremely low self-esteem. Because they don't have a good set of life skills, the internalized issues get overwhelming to the point a child may develop an internal fantasy world that is far from normal reality. When they do this, there sometimes comes a time when they actually try to act out the fantasy either alone or in tandem with another Transitional Child.

Transitional Children are generally in their teen years or early twenties. They started out fairly normal in appearance and actions but over time began to turn more and more inward. This is because Transitional Children feel everything extremely deeply. Unfortunately since this isn't an obvious development, the depth of their feelings goes unnoticed by those around them. Such children in all of their sensitivities, begin to close off due to the intensity. As this happens, they may self-medicate, possibly with drugs and/or alcohol, and after a time, they may get so closed off from their feelings the only way they can feel anything is to hurt themselves—often via self-mutilation, commonly known these days as cutting.

Transitional Children are overly private about everything. If they talk about things it is usually in short sentences or very superficially, not revealing anything. Or, they might make random remarks that seem to be kidding but may reveal a much darker internal dialogue. These kids just feel different, set off from everyone else, even damaged.

The issue here is that in the evolutionary process, there is always trial and error on the part of creation since it is clearly responsive to the signals it receives from everything created. Everything is in flux. As one thing changes into a different something, new arrangements of energy spring up until the process streamlines. The Transitional Children got much of the sensitivity without the coping mechanisms to use and disperse the emotionally powerful stimuli. As caregivers we honestly didn't catch this. These kids are so darned good at hiding it.

If left untreated or unacknowledged, Transitional Children may descend into a place of darkness that does not seem to have an escape. There have been a huge number of suicides among teenagers of late. I have worked with many families who have been victims of terrible, sad outcomes as their Transitional Children opted out of life, believing they were so flawed that there was no way to remedy this.

The Transitional Children need to learn how to bring their feelings outside of themselves. They need strong guidance but at the same time the freedom to expand. What

I mean by this is that too many rules and diagnoses can leave Transitional Children feeling so trapped they will do anything to get out. Teaching them to bring their feelings out in the open must begin at a very young age to avoid altogether the darker aspects of being a Transitional. In our everyday world we are so busy, so over-obligated, that we often miss the subtleties around us. With the Transitional Children, subtleties may be all we get. It is this group I will be writing about in a later chapter when I talk about why young people are susceptible to fantasy and some are committing such desperate and heinous acts in schools and other public places.

Our Beautiful Silent Ones

The most endearing group of the Children of Now is our Beautiful Silent Ones as I call them. These children are afflicted with physical disabilities and seem at a glance to be noncommunicative and barely present at all. But when we look closer, they are living love.

These kids cannot or do not speak, but somehow they manage to get across what it is they need to say. How? They do it telepathically. When I first encountered this phenomenon when I was just beginning to discover the Children of Now, I began by hearing phrases, giggles in my head, and more than one voice becoming more and more active and then overlapping. I truly thought I was losing it. But what I heard not only made sense, the words were often profound about love, humanity, matters of the heart beyond everyday thinking, and they seemed to be coming from nowhere.

I was traveling at that time for seven weeks straight, speaking at conferences all over the United States, and my schedule was crazy busy. One day when they were all talking at once, I couldn't think my own thoughts. It seemed that my mind was full of them and had no room for me. I remember frustratingly spouting two sentiments that day. The first was "If you are real, start showing up in person because this is getting insane!" The second was "And if you *are* real, as soon as I get home I will start writing down everything you are saying, but for now, I really need to concentrate on what I am doing!"

Silence.

Silence.

And then their messages began to clarify. They were amazing. And they were the impetus for my book, *The Children of Now*.

About three weeks after I returned home, my phone rang. On the other end was a woman who seems apologetic, and through her giggles, said that our appointment wasn't for her, it was for her son Weston. And then I started to laugh. Without thinking how bizarre it would sound, I asked her if he was one of the children who had been talking to me telepathically.

"Oh yes! He has been known to do that! He doesn't speak, but he told me to contact you."

"How did he do that?"

"He pulled up your website and pointed to your picture."

Long story short, Weston turned out to be the most powerful telepath I have known to date. He had a great time taking over my thoughts and putting pictures and movies in my head of the realities he wanted me to see. They could be quite entertaining but also at times a nuisance as it made it very difficult for me to concentrate on anything!

A couple of months after I met Weston, I was in Scottsdale, Arizona, to present at the Celebrate Your Life Conference. Between lectures, I was standing in the lobby talking to a friend. My back was to the aisle, and suddenly I heard in my head "Hi, I made it!" in the sweetest little voice. I froze momentarily, not knowing whom I would encounter when I turned around, but also knowing it was another of the children who had been talking to me.

When I faced her, I saw a shining light. She was a slight little thing with flowing red hair and the hugest crystal blue eyes you can imagine. Her mom Karen was with her, pushing her wheelchair. Karen introduced me to Lorrin, and even though we already knew each other, it was a trip meeting her in person. Lorrin for all intents and purposes was nonfunctional in her body. She couldn't move except for a little in her arms and her head. But honestly, Lorrin seemed to glow. She radiated pure love like nothing I had ever seen.

That night Lorrin managed to keep me awake most of the time with images of her dancing ballet in a room of mirrored walls. As I watched in awe, she told me not to feel sorry for her because she really was free anytime she wanted. She said that her favorite thing to do was dance and that maybe someday her physical body would catch up.

Over the next few months I also met Nicholas and Tristan through their parents. Each had different physical issues and each was nonverbal but powerfully telepathic. It is funny how things can be, but when each one of these kids popped in on me, I could tell who they were by how they felt. Weston was a powerhouse, strong and always in motion. Lorrin felt like a gentle breeze, Nicholas quite fragile, and Tristan tentative but sure. Tristan is an extremely high-frequency Star Kid, and when his mom and I talked, Tristan was right there showing me what I needed to know.

There were others too. I was invited up to Bemidji, Minnesota, right after Hurricane Katrina. There, in a small lake, lie the headwaters of the Mississippi River. Powerful Native American chiefs and medicine people had gathered there to do a ceremony to heal the river and all of the lands along it. They were concerned about an imbalance in the earth and had come to correct it with ceremony. It was a true honor to be asked to help.

As we sat around talking, my hostess showed me a clay bowl that she had bought from the grandfather of the child who had made it. The markings on the bowl were out if this world. They were mathematically arranged in a pattern that seemed to communicate something. As I observed the markings, I began to hear a new child. He said his name was Brian. Feeling comfortable in the assembled group, I began to relay to them the messages Brian was bringing to me. He spoke of another time and place that no longer existed. His descriptions were exact and his emotions raw. He was a soul who had experienced many lifetimes. Listening to him was moving to the core.

As Brian gave us what he had to say, he said that he was in the area. I suggested that since I didn't live there, he show up for one of the local people in our assembled group and they would help him. Not much later he appeared in person to the daughter of our hostess, and they hit it off.

The Children of Now seem to embody time and space on levels we can only imagine. When the Beautiful Silent Ones travel out of body, they cross all perceived barriers of when and where. They do so gleefully because they have found a way to be free of their physical limitations.

Once I began to write about this spectacular group of beings, people all over the world began hearing different children telepathically. As first I thought it was the power of suggestion at work. But later, as people emailed me word for word or called and repeated things to me that one child or another had said directly to me, I could no longer doubt the massive phenomenon. Our Beautiful Silent Ones aren't so silent after all.

Having encountered a number of these special beings, I learned a powerful life lesson. When we are growing up, we are taught to look away from what is different, dysfunctional, or broken. I have found that doing so is the greatest mistake anyone can possibly make. To be touched in the heart by a different type of voice is to be touched by the greatest, purest love of all, that which is innocent and unedited. It will mark your soul forever.

Please, don't look away ever again. There is a jewel in there waiting to make you a very rich person. You just have to listen with the right ears—the ears of your heart!

Angels on Earth

The smallest group of the Children of Now is the Angels on Earth. They are also one of the most fragile. They seem to feel the weight of the world all of the time, knowing deep inside that all is holy. They also feel as if there is something they must do but they can't figure out what. They are intrinsically sad.

They just know they have wings and are frustrated that others can't see them. It makes them feel set apart from everyone else because they are so different. Their wings seem to reside in another reality just outside of ours. Their wings are blue or salmon-colored, brown or gray, for the most part. These children feel everything.

One young Angel on Earth I encountered called me for advice on the recommendation of someone he had met. He had been walking barefoot all over the planet, trying to figure out what it was he was supposed to do.

"Live," I told him. "Have the experiences you are here to have and the rest will be revealed to you in the process. Take care of you. You aren't. Your physical body has needs that aren't being met. Drying up and disappearing won't do anything but waste the myriad of opportunities that you have to make a difference. Sometimes that difference is only in your heart. Sometimes that is all that is needed."

Another Angel on Earth came to me for a healing session through her mother. As she lay on the table and I worked through her etheric system, all of a sudden blue wings spread before me. Honestly, I was pretty startled!

I asked her, "Do you know you have wings?"

"Yes, but no one but me can see them."

Testing, I asked, "Do you know what color they are?"

"Blue. Sky blue."

"But," she said, "No one can see them. I got so frustrated by this I had them tattooed on my back."

So I told her, "I can see them . . ."

She sat up and pulled up her top and sure enough, she had inked sky blue wings that covered the entirety of her back. They were a serious work of art.

My new friend was thrilled that I could see her wings and knew about those things. She and I talked at length, and I did my best to counsel her about her feelings and awareness. She could see beyond our reality and often had spirits and other beings around her. This frightened her. It seemed as if she had her own United Nations of otherworldly beings. Of course they all wanted her help, but she wasn't in an emotional place to take that on. She needed to heal herself first. I worked with her off and on for years, and we managed to make some great progress. Her mom was terrific and very supportive of her daughter's strange journey.

For Angels on Earth life can be a struggle. Most have to learn to have the sense of self missing in the younger ones I have met. Angels on Earth seem to be here to heal themselves. Somehow in doing that they turn things around and try to help everyone else. That is unless they fold. Some of them are just too fragile to be here. If they are able to move through their challenges, they come out the other end strong and powerful. They learn to flex their wings and exert their power, to wrap them around another, to share immense compassion and healing, or to hold them gently on their backs as wisdom comes forward, and to silently stand vigil while another learns the power of their soul.

Angels on Earth, if they are aware of who they are, require a great deal of support from those they love. Finding the self buried under all that sadness can be a serious challenge, but they can do it.

CHAPTER 3

How Do We Know What's Real and What Is Imagination?

The Children of Now come out with the darndest things, and some of them frighten parents. All kids have wild imaginations, and sometimes it is hard to know what is real and what isn't. But with this amazing group of children one never knows what will be next! They don't have the usual filters in place. Their awareness may encompass many layers of reality that we as adults don't have access to, and so it is really hard to imagine that they may in fact be seeing or hearing things in worlds beyond ours.

There are some common things that the Children of Now are known to say or do. Of course, things vary with each child, but the subject matter, although seemingly bizarre, is part of their everyday reality.

Here are some great examples. What do you think, are they true or false?

QUESTION: Your baby is sitting in your shopping basket at Walmart. While you are preoccupied, he has locked eyes with another person. He never breaks his gaze and appears to know this person who is a complete stranger to you. True or false: Is there something happening here?

ANSWER: True. As infants and toddlers, the Children of Now often maintain some of their memories from before they were born. It is not at all uncommon for them to recognize how another person looks or feels. When they lock onto someone like this, they are resonating together with that person. Underneath it all a silent meeting of souls is taking place, if only for a moment. This can be a powerful experience for both the little one and the recipient of the gaze.

QUESTION: "Mommy there are angels in the room!" True of false?

ANSWER: True. Angels are commonly seen and described by the Children of Now, particularly when the children are toddlers. When my granddaughter was about a year and a half old, she would point at different parts of the ceiling and describe the angels as male or female and tell me the colors of their garments or the energy surrounding them and sometimes even why they were there.

QUESTION: "I remember talking to God about coming here." True or false?

ANSWER: True. This is a common comment from the Children of Now. They often describe what it was like to sit with God and plan their new lives.

QUESTION: "I use to be a pilot in an airplane. We shot people in other airplanes down, and then one day my plane got shot down too." Or "I was on a boat out in the ocean, and there was fire everywhere. Everyone was dying around me. I tried really hard to hold on but the ship sank." True or false?

ANSWER: This may seem like the child watches too much TV, but the truth is that there are countless stories about the Children of Now remembering every detail of their immediate past lives even to the point that their previous identity can be verified. One boy whom I talked about in *The Children of Now* and his little friend, both six years old, remembered being in a closet in a hotel with big paddle fans and open rooms with potted palms everywhere. They were hiding from some "bad men" in that closet, who came in and shot them. They remembered dying together. The parents, intrigued by the details in their stories, started searching and found the actual incident and location the boys had described.

QUESTION: "A lady comes into my room at night and talks to me." True or false?

ANSWER: True. The Children of Now can often see the spirits of people who have died but stay around for various reasons (such as the need to tell someone something or a task left unfinished). They seem to know when people on the earth plane have the ability to see them and so tend to gravitate toward the Children of Now. The spirits are generally harmless. Sometimes deceased relatives come to watch over the child while others have messages for other loved ones.

QUESTION: "There is a man who comes and talks to me when I am out in the yard. No one else can see him. He is really lonely." True or false?

ANSWER: True. Spirits can be attached to other people, land, buildings, or even objects. Often when there is a wandering spirit such as this, he will have had a home nearby and have suffered some kind of loss, like the death of a relative or spouse, or he may have passed away and not known to go on home, so to speak.

QUESTION: "I have an invisible friend and she loves to play with me." True or false?

ANSWER: True. Because the Children of Now can see into other planes of reality, they may share any number of descriptions of their invisible friends from those other realities. They may be tiny people or from another planet or of the spirit world, in fact from anywhere but here! Others commonly hear their children talking in strange languages to seemingly no one. There is someone there, but with all of our general defenses, we just don't see them. Our everyday defenses cause tension in our energy fields and trigger those filters to stay in place and keep us from seeing into other planes of reality. Again, this is a harmless situation.

QUESTION: "There are people watching me in my bed." True or false?

ANSWER: Quite true for many of the Children of Now. Because these kids resonate at higher and different frequencies than most of the rest of us, they are like beacons in creation. There are many "out there" who are curious and come to observe the kids. They don't touch them or hurt them; they just watch. Sometimes they come in multiples. There are many stories about four doglike humanoid forms who come and just stare at the kids. They can be terrifying to see but are harmless. This kind of event is often the cause of night terrors which may encompass not only the bedroom but, for some reason, also the bathroom. This is far different from the imaginary monster in the closet!

QUESTION: "Everyone has light around them, and when people move, the lights change color." True or false?

ANSWER: True. Some Children of Now can see the auric field and describe the colors and field dynamics to a tee. This is a real gift because a lot can be discerned from what is happening in that part of our energy system.

QUESTION: "I remember picking you as my mommy before I came." True or false?

ANSWER: True. Boundless accounts from the Children of Now describe the moment they chose their parents and often why. If a child will be physically challenged in this lifetime, she will choose a parent who will nurture her or has something deep to learn. The children may describe choosing a parent who will challenge them so that they can learn specific skills or attributes. Whatever their reason, it is always sincere and well stated.

QUESTION: "I can fly!" True or false?

ANSWER: True. While for many of us, dreams of flying are common—and they are for children as well—the Children of Now easily travel out of body. When they do that, because they are not weighed down by a physical nature, their experiences feel a lot like flying.

QUESTION: "There are people who follow me around all of the time. They are not all the same. Some look nice and others scare me." True or false?

ANSWER: Although less common than other visitations, this can also be true. This particular circumstance tends to happen more with teens than with the smaller kids. Particularly if the child is self-medicating with drugs or alcohol, he may attract negative types of beings. These are usually parasitic and thrive on the negative emotions of the child. At the same time though, there are often others with them. These are guardians who keep the child safe. Think of this like any small crowd: as with all groups, some folks are really nice while others not so much.

QUESTION: "Let me touch him; I can make him feel better." True or false?

ANSWER: True. The Children of Now seem to have an innate understanding of the energy field and how it is affected when we don't feel well or are injured. Often the child won't say a word, but will just go over to the affected person and lay hands on them. Usually that person will feel much better after the child's touch. A related but different type of situation may happen when these children move to music. They may move slowly and deliberately, often with their eyes closed. They are certainly enjoying the music, but they are also working with energy at the same time. My granddaughter had a masterful command of energy and to watch her was like watching a tai chi master.

QUESTION: "Fairies like peanut butter!" True or false?

ANSWER: LOL false! Just kidding here; who knows what fairies like to eat! The point is that the Children of Now will tell you things that challenge your reality. Listen deeply and don't be too quick to judge. Give them a chance to tell you the whole story. Sometimes their imaginations are hard at play, while other times they are having very real experiences. Just because we don't understand them, doesn't mean they aren't real!

These are just a few everyday types of examples of situations one may encounter with the Children of Now. There is no reason to be afraid of these kinds of comments or events. These things and more are simply part of who our Children of Now are and what they can do. I have received hundreds if not thousands of emails from parents or caregivers who are terrified that something is wrong with their child because they said something like what I listed above or witnessed the child in some of these situations.

There is absolutely nothing wrong with your child if any of these things or something similar occurs.

I repeat:

There is absolutely nothing wrong with your child if any of these things or something similar occurs.

They are simply being who they are! And who they are is beautiful!

Usually by age seven or eight the child will begin to lose some of these very natural abilities. Why? Because by then they are in such fully encompassing social settings as school, and they begin to defend themselves due to peer pressure, rules and regulations, bullies, and any number of other situations. That background defense system creates a thickening in the energy field and begins to cloud the child's access to otherworld realities.

Children who are home-schooled or in circumstances that allow for expression of their creative being and do not try to force them into a mold are often able to maintain their psi gifts into adolescence and beyond.

One of the worst things we can do when something weird comes up with our kids is to tell them that whatever it is isn't real. Yes it is. Just because we don't see the world from the same set of eyes our children do doesn't mean that what they are sharing with us isn't real. And no, they aren't mentally whacked either. They are simply being who they are.

It is vitally important to support these kids in their strangeness. Don't pretend to understand, because the child will know you are lying. Just honor the child. Ask questions about the experience. If she has a spirit visiting that no one seems to recognize (i.e., not a relative), tell the child to ask what the spirit needs. Maybe it is something very simple, and once stated, they will go away.

A different sort of mistake I have seen to varying degrees is when some parents recognize the giftedness of these kids and put them on a pedestal. This is understandable when a kid is spouting the wisdom of the ages; it is hard to grasp that this is normal. But putting them on a pedestal does an extreme disservice to the children. They need a structure, a framework, and guidance about how to live in our world. They are still children no matter what they can do. We must not place them in any situation where they are expected to be otherwise.

Some years ago I was speaking at a conference, and in the vendor area there was a ten-year-old child manning a booth. His parents had him doing readings for people because of his intuitive nature, and they were charging for the readings too. All of that might have been okay, but the boy was exhausted. He was being overworked to the nth degree. He didn't get time to eat. He didn't get any breaks. He was trapped by his own parents and a victim of his own gifts. Honestly, I was furious. Setting a child up like this is not okay. Forget labor laws and all of the social protections that are in place; the Children of Now have not come here to be exploited or put on display. They have a much greater agenda, which we will talk about a bit later.

Another issue that comes up is a lack of discipline. The parents experience their child speaking of knowing God, of having amazing otherworldly experiences, and so they don't feel comfortable instilling the normal discipline given to most kids. Instead, there seems to be an unspoken expectation that the child knows everything. This can mean that the child is often disruptive in public, even to the point of rudeness.

No matter who they are and what their abilities children need a good solid framework so that they feel safe. They need to learn everything every child needs to learn. They also need to recognize and understand interpersonal boundaries as well as how to behave in public and private places.

When kids have boundaries and know what to expect, they thrive. They feel safe. Not only that but they develop a healthy ego from their interactions.

CHAPTER 4

Autism, ADD, ADHD, and More

Why include a chapter about this subject? When I first began to delve into the Children of Now as a subject, I really thought the topic only covered our magically gifted kids and perhaps the Bridge Generation. But as I stepped out into the public sphere to present to audiences all that I had learned, certain other issues kept coming up. I realized over time that there is an entirely other dimension to this phenomenon. This includes autism, Asperger's, attention deficit disorder, attention deficit hyperactivity disorder, and other perceived ailments.

I don't look at autism, ADD, ADHD, or even Asperger's as diseases. Instead what I see is a darker flip side of our magical children's experiences. The children referenced in this chapter are just as exceptional and just as magical. In fact, they often begin as perfect babies and are later influenced to become something else. In this chapter I will discuss why we have an epidemic of seemingly broken children who are not broken. Instead, they are differently abled. We will also learn why there appears to be such a large spectrum of effects.

The sensitivities and subtle energy fields of the Children of Now are easily affected in myriad ways. Sometimes, due to the ignorance of society, pharmaceutical companies, and even manufacturers, the sensitivities of these very special little ones are exponentially impacted by vaccines, chemicals, drugs, toxins, heavy metals, and other contributing factors that cause a perfect child to become something different. If we are to understand and address the epidemic of such "disorders" rampant in today's world, we must begin to understand the causes from different perspectives than we currently take.

ADD and ADHD

Attention deficit disorder (ADD) and attention deficit hyperactivity disorder (ADHD) have become household words. Children are constantly being labeled with one or another of these diagnoses because they flit around, won't sit still, and do not appear to be paying attention. The Children of Now don't do these things because they are misbehaving. They are sensitive to everything—color, sound, what is in their visual field, what assaults their hearing, what they feel from others as they pick up the emotions and motivations from everyone around them. We introduce them into environments and expectations based on an old paradigm, and they just cannot cope.

With an onslaught of outside forces battering their senses, these kids have to move around to avoid getting overloaded. For instance, in the school setting, every wall, every shelf, every cabinet, and every tabletop is covered with supplies, posters, papers the kids have done, and sentiments about what they can achieve. The furniture is usually hard, unyielding wood or metal, and the room itself is institutional with drab colors and hard concrete or plaster surfaces. The space is filled with little people and a teacher as well as possibly a teacher's assistant. Every single person in the room is experiencing feelings and perceptions. They are happy or sad, comfortable or anxious; they are or are not getting what they need or may be having trouble at home or with other students. There are voices, movement, environmental input in the background such as people in the hallways or outside of the windows.

To the Children of Now, all of these factors add up to a cacophony of input beyond what they can bear. When a child (or anyone) is energy sensitive, moving around helps dissipate specific energies. For me, when I am in a crowd of people, I move about constantly so that I can avoid any buildup. The kids do the same thing. Unfortunately when they do it, they are seen as overactive, misbehaving, or even unmanageable.

Perhaps they don't need to be managed. Maybe instead they just need to be understood.

This can happen at home too. Kids tend to have every toy they ever owned, a multitude of stuffed animals, or other things in their rooms. Often their things are in disarray all over the place. And of course everyone at home has their feelings and experiences. The Children of Now are also sensitive to those. If there is discord, it is not uncommon for these kids to have a serious meltdown, sometimes even to the point that they short-circuit or have seizures. But no medical cause generally shows up when they get tested.

Out in society, all is chaos to the senses of the Children of Now. There is so much input, so many modalities of information, things to see, to feel, to live, to learn, that they often become victims of aural and visual overload. When children get to that point, they act out.

The Children of Now don't think like the adults around them. Instead, they think compartmentally, being able to file away fragments of information for later until they all make sense. It means they try to handle large amounts of information by separating it into compartments in their brains, which becomes a problem when there is too much stimuli to pack in for later processing. Moving around helps to avoid overload.

Their minds are like lightning storms. So much happens so fast it is all like a flash. Compared to the Children of Now, our minds are like molasses in a mudflow. By the time we realize anything, the kids have moved on exponentially to a dozen other things. They have retained it all, too.

It is scientifically proven that the brain perceives much sooner than we realize. By the time we act on a perception it is old news. These kids don't have that hesitation. They process data immeasurable fast. It follows that their bodies are simply trying to keep up. Unfortunately societies' answer is to medicate the kids or sanction them somehow for their behaviors. Instead of deciding we know they are not paying attention, if we ask them about their day and their perceptions, they would express deep awareness of how everyone around them seemed to experience their days. They would express much deeper knowledge about what was taught that day, taking the teachings further into application and even examples of how to use what they have learned. It's just that they aren't interested in the old ways of doing things.

Why Autism Is a Spectrum

Unfortunately when talking about the Children of Now, the conversation must also include the topic of autism. The online *Merriam-Webster Dictionary* defines autism as

au · tism noun \ˈȯ-ˌtiz-əm\
: a developmental disorder that appears by age three and that is variable in expression but is recognized and diagnosed by impairment of the ability to form normal social relationships, by impairment of the ability to communicate with others, and by stereotyped behavior patterns especially as exhibited by a preoccupation with repetitive activities of restricted focus rather than with flexible and imaginative ones.

According to current statistics, autism has reached epidemic proportions. It is not at all understood, and there doesn't seem to be any way to prevent it from occurring. According to the Centers for Disease Control and Prevention (CDC), one in every fifty children will have autism with more of the afflicted being boys. The answer to understanding autism may be within energy fields. Modern medicine does not take into account that it is now scientifically provable and measurable that human beings, in fact all living things, have subtle energy fields that have weight and emit light energy. How much light and how large the field is are different from one individual to another.

While I am not a medical doctor, I have the ability to see the body and its energy fields and am a well-known medical intuitive. I teach a certification course called Touching the Light based on my book of the same name (Weiser Books, 2011). In the course, I relate energy dynamics to the etheric anatomy and how energy anomalies affect the entire life experience as well as the health of the subject. These levels of energy are palpable and changeable and can be influenced in certain ways to create change and therefore potential improvements in health and other aspects of life.

The palpability of our energy field is directly related to why we lose on average around twenty-one grams when we pass away and shed our bodies. Our consciousness, our soul, adds physical mass to our bodies when they are animated, or shall we say, alive. When our subtle energy no longer inhabits our body, the body literally loses the weight of our living energy.

In fact, we have an entire etheric anatomy that is very intricate with lots of layers and power centers that all work together to keep us healthy and in touch with our intuitive nature as well. Our etheric anatomy encompasses multiple dimensions of reality, and each and every area of our subtle energy field has a job to do. This is our first line of defense from being affected energetically. It is our detector system. When the subtle energy field is impacted by outside stimuli, the external area of our field can become enlarged, misshapen, even misplaced.

The Children of Now are hypersensitive to things that can affect their energy fields because they function innately at higher frequencies than previous generations. Higher frequencies mean finer, lighter energy. The finer and lighter the energy, the more easily it is influenced.

For years children's required vaccines contained substances such as mercury. There is also mercury in our fish as well as in the overall environment. Mercury is conductive and has even been studied for use as a fuel in interstellar travel. Our bodies are also susceptible to heavy metal poisoning from various sources including but not limited to plumbing pipes, household products, older paints, and environmental chemicals. It is also likely that genetically modified foods and chemicals as well as other toxins found in our environment are contributing to the autism epidemic.

When even a minute amount of mercury, thimerosal, or another conductive substance is introduced into a physical body, the subtle energy system responds by expanding or rerouting its normal flow patterns. As it does, other aspects of the subtle energy system are pushed out of normal alignment, and overall functioning is impaired. The challenges presented may be physical, mental, emotional, or consciousness-based, and we may even be affected on levels outside of the physical realm.

Because consciousness is literally part of the subtle energy field, consciousness can be affected. There may even be changes that occur in the energy field that literally misplace the consciousness from the body. When that happens, the child is disconnected, won't make eye contact, and is often nonverbal. When the misplacement takes on certain more profound dynamics energetically, what we get is the savant. A savant is someone who is profoundly brilliant at a specific task like counting or playing classical piano.

Our external field is also affected by electromagnetic emissions in our environment. Some examples of this may include electronics such as computers, cell phones, medical equipment, electric power lines, in fact anything that uses energy in any way may throw off the excess or by-products of that usage. Our fields pick up errant patterning that can later become literal dysfunction due to how that foreign energy has influenced our finely attuned energy systems. We can also pick up energetic dross or junk.

Think of this much like having a splinter in your skin. It is uncomfortable at first, but it doesn't shut you down. Energetic junk is the same way. The longer the anomaly is in our field, the more the field adapts to its presence. In the same way that our bodies will eventually encapsulate that splinter, making it hard to find, our external energy fields wall off foreign energy. This causes interference in our flow patterns so that the energies reroute, as they seek the truest, easiest path of functioning. In fact every part of our etheric anatomy will adapt, refine, or change to avoid dysfunction. Sometimes those adaptations actually create worse issues.

Note the five figures in these pages. Though simplified, they are quite accurate in their representations of different situations. Figure 2 denotes a normal healthy external field.

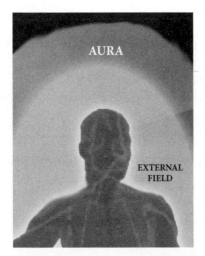

Figure 2: *Normal external field*

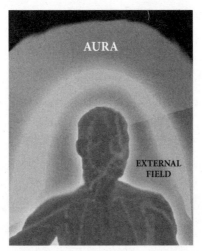

Figure 3: *Misplaced external field*

Figure 3 shows how, due to influences not natural to the body, the field can become misplaced or separated from the body. A gap is left between the consciousness and the body. Because of the gap, consciousness cannot be fully present in the body. There may be moments of apparent presence, but they cannot be maintained. This is why an autistic child often does not make eye contact or appears to be in another world. He just might be. How far the field moves determines where on the spectrum an autistic child is diagnosed and how affected that child is.

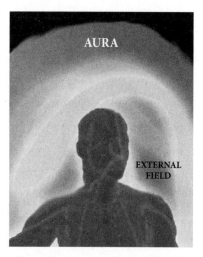

Figure 4: *Fragmented external field*

In some cases an energetic bridge can be created between the physical and the misplaced external field. Since this type of work is in the subtle realm, often the effects can be slow to show themselves, but ultimately changes can occur. In other cases the results can be immediate and profound.

One case I worked on concerned a four-year-old little guy who had never spoken. In his case I was clearly able to see the gap between the physical and his consciousness. I created an energy bridge, and immediately after the session when he and his mom were in the car going somewhere, the little guy piped up from the backseat and said, "I love you, Mommy." She nearly wrecked the car in her excitement! This technique does not always work, but it has been known to effect great change over time. The results are dependent on a number of factors such as the harmonics of the child and the environmental situation the child is in among others.

Figure 5: *Multidimensional aspects (normal)*

Figure 4 displays a fragmented external field. This type of abnormality in the energy field can cause unpredictable periodic symptoms such as being really present one minute to off in space another. In extremely severe cases, this type of anomaly may even cause symptoms of schizophrenia or even multiple personality disorder. When the field fragments, sometimes parts of the consciousness get stuck in the moment of dysfunction and stay there.

In its efforts to normalize in the system, the consciousness may literally be jumping from one fragmented aspect to another. Or, there may be such a wide gap between the

Figure 6: *Multiple dimensional aspects where the external field has overlaid more than one timeline*

fragments that the consciousness has no place to go but to an empty space. Since there is no natural bridge from the body to any of the fragments, outer changes or limitations may be profound.

In some cases the fragmentation can be assimilated into a more normal, singularly working system. This is done by pulling all of the fragmented sections together and reharmonizing them as one strong unit of energy.

Figure 5 shows how we have many different aspects all living simultaneously in different levels of reality. These aspects follow a timeline of past, present, and future, and all exist simultaneously. The timeline is a living record of all that we have ever been and done, are, and will be. Shamans often track a person's timeline to find the root of a current problem, illness, or issue.

When the external field moves or becomes fragmented, the consciousness may become more active on a different level of reality, thus depriving the current reality, the child, of normal awareness and attentiveness. Figure 6 shows how, when the subtle energy is pushed out of its normal alignments, consciousness is not only in the body in our world, but also overlays all or parts of other dimensional aspects of consciousness. The external field can often be adjusted to a corrected size and shape. This is done via a method of calibration of the energies in which they literally change their patterning, resulting in an alteration in size and density.

The dynamics of the subtle energy field are exactly why we have a spectrum of autism rather than a specific predictable level of autism. Each person is harmonically different. Each of us is energetically made up of different frequencies that come together to make us. Our individual sets of frequencies are unique in all of creation. No one is exactly like us. It would be impossible. No two same frequencies can occupy the same space; they will cancel each other out. It is for this reason that early cloning attempts failed as the DNA began to break down and the cloned subjects died.

Autism can range from the barely affected to the seriously afflicted. At the same time as there are consciousness issues with autism, there are also often digestive and autoimmune issues. When the body has issues, they are nearly always harmonically related, and the digestive tract is harmonically the lowest frequency system in our body. Harmonically speaking, when there is dysfunction, the densest areas are the first to begin to decay, or in easier terms, to malfunction. Since most of our autoimmune support lives in our intestinal tract, as the digestive tract becomes challenged, so does the autoimmune system.

As demonstrated here, there are a number of contributing factors to problems in autism that are never even considered by the modern medical community. It is sad that something so relatively simple is denied in treatment.

What causes autism is still up for speculation. There is no singular known cause, but there do seem to be contributing factors such as GMOs and elements in vaccinations or even our environment. We will look at some of these factors more closely in later chapters.

Asperger's

Asperger's is another part of the autism spectrum. Trying to relate to children with Asperger's can be infuriating. Their methods of interacting are very different from most people, and they do not follow normal social cues so they can appear indifferent or uncaring. That is hardly the truth. In fact, it is often their high level of internal sensitivity that leads to them protecting themselves by internalizing everything.

People with Asperger's (as many adults have been diagnosed with it as well) encompass a range of functioning from low to high. High-functioning people with Asperger's likely hold down a good professional job and may make great engineers or techs. Asperger's kids, if treated early, can go on to live very productive lives. They can be excellent as scientists, historians, or in other technically oriented careers. Their interests are narrow, but they know everything there is to know within that range.

Since this is a relatively new diagnosis, included below are many of the symptoms one may find in a person with Asperger's. Symptoms vary, but this provides a good framework and information on where to get further details.

Some of the Symptoms of Asperger's

- There is an inflexibility and attachment to routines. People with Asperger's feel as if they are in their safety zone within a predictable routine. If the routine is altered or not followed, the person may suffer an emotional upset or cause disturbances.

- People with Asperger's are quite fixed in their habits and often display repetitive rituals and behaviors. This can be observed in such body movements, habits, and behaviors as hand flapping, twirling, rocking, or obscure methods of play.

- Often people with Asperger's can have difficulty instigating or engaging in conversations as well as maintaining eye contact with the other person. Conversation tends to revolve around obsessively discussing the subject *they* are extremely interested in. If people with Asperger's aren't interested in the subject the other person brings up, they may simply walk away or not reply at all.

- People with Asperger's are not always able to read the emotional cues most of us see in the faces and body language of others. In fact, they do not often understand the difference between what is a thought and what is a feeling.

- They have limited social skills and may often be considered rude.

- Often people with Asperger's have a tendency to isolate and difficulties in developing and keeping close friendships.

- It is common for people with Asperger's to have a very low sensitivity to the emotions of others.

- They have difficulty understanding both their own emotions and the emotions of others. It can also be common for them to have extreme emotional responses to what seems to others to be a minor event or trigger.

- People with Asperger's exhibit a hypersensitivity to sound. For those with Asperger's, sound can act as an irritant. Even sounds that seem small or insignificant to others can act as a trigger for the person to become agitated.

- People with Asperger's may have impaired motor skills. This doesn't apply to all cases. There may be problems with the motor skills required for playing catch, riding a bike, or tying shoelaces. This is often seen in autistic kids as well.

A full list of Asperger's symptoms can be found at www.asperger-advice.com. My experience has been that the people behind this site are very supportive and informative.

Loving a person with Asperger's can be challenging since the relationship dynamics most of us are accustomed to using do not apply with someone who is inherently logical and not prone to the emotional. Imagine trying to have a passionate, deeply emotional conversation with Mr. Spock of *Star Trek*. But it is possible to learn to adapt.

CHAPTER 5

The Drugging of the Innocent

We have learned that the Children of Now have extensive sensitivities. They can easily get overwhelmed due to visual or audio overload. For instance, if there is too much clutter or too many objects in the visual field, it can be disturbing on an internal level to the sensitive child. The child will likely become agitated or act out not understanding the cause of the discomfort.

At the same time, in different institutional environments such as a school setting that are full of hard surfaces with no rugs or carpet, the sound bounces around a lot and there are extraneous noises that are distracting. A Child of Now may find it overwhelming to maintain a focus on any one thing. Too many types of sound all at the same time can feel to Crystalline Children as if they are being pummeled by outside forces.

Because of these environmental issues, the Children of Now fidget a lot as a way to move the energy and to get it to flow faster. People who are energetically sensitive do not tend to stay in one place for very long at a time. As they stand still, energy builds up and becomes uncomfortable.

Moving around brings the energetically sensitive greater comfort.

Or if the external stimuli are overwhelming, the child may become disruptive because he doesn't understand why he is so uncomfortable. Of course, all of this is done on subconscious levels and rarely ever intentional.

Some adults may experience something similar if they are very sensitive. For instance, walking into a big-box store like Walmart or Best Buy, or . . . well, you get my drift. There is so much stuff piled so high that it can be difficult to spot anything. Quickly the sensitive person becomes visually overloaded and often will leave or avoid the store in the future. In those same places, sound has its own dynamics. There may be music playing, people talking, forklifts or other store equipment in operation, announcements for specials, cash registers going, and more and more and more. Suffice it to say that audio overload is imminent for the sensitive person.

Now on top of that, imagine that you are required to sit still, look forward, and pay attention only to the person who is across the store from you. You must listen to that person no matter what, and if you are distracted or not paying attention, there will be consequences. It won't be long before you are feeling not only frustrated but a little insane at the same time.

Due to the behavioral issues often experienced with the Children of Now, these kids are more often than not put into categories for medical or psychiatric diagnoses such as

ADD, ADHD, or even bipolar disorder. After that, many of these children are given medications for a wide range of symptoms and in varying dosages. Many of these meds are intended for adults and are not proven or deemed safe for children. In addition, some of the drugs actually *cause* psychiatric symptoms, and as a result, the children get worse instead of better.

Using medications to "normalize" kids has become an unfortunate standard practice. The drugs usually dull down the Children of Now and inhibit their natural ability to process energy buildup. This can lead to depression or other symptoms and take what was a differently normal child down a path of low self-esteem.

Parents of some of the Children of Now whom I have worked with have told me hair-raising stories about how a child's school demanded a child be medicated or expelled. One mother contacted me when the school sent social services to her door, saying that her child must be drugged or he would be taken away from her. Other medical personnel who work both in doctor's offices and at hospitals, particularly in the northeastern United States where big pharma has a huge presence, have told me multiple stories of how the pharmaceutical companies reward both the schools and physicians' offices for selling their drugs.

Although it is supposed to be illegal for the drug companies to give kickbacks, apparently they get creative about how to compensate those who propagate the use of their products. I heard one story from medical personnel about a drug company paying for an administrator's son's birthday party. The bill was for an ungodly amount in excess of a hundred thousand dollars. I have been told other stories about new boats and other expensive perks offered for the same reasons. All of these incidents were told to me over time by actual employees of the medical offices and physicians. One had worked at a pharmaceutical company but left because she couldn't in good conscience participate in or support these underhanded drug sales activities.

In some cases schools were being rewarded financially for recommending the medication of children. One witness reported that they were rewarded on a per child basis; i.e., there was a set amount of money given per child referred to drug therapy. While I have no concrete way to confirm these allegations, they were brought to me unsolicited numerous times by multiple sources as I traveled and lectured about the Children of Now or taught workshops on the subject by medical or pharmaceutical personnel who witnessed the situations firsthand and were in no way connected with each other. Many of them were in my classes and lectures looking for a better way to take care of these unique children without hurting them. There was no apparent need or agenda to misinform the public, simply a strong desire for change.

If these stories are true, and I personally have no doubt that they are, they indicate a huge financial force behind the drugging of so many kids.

The saddest thing of all is that many, many of the Children of Now need no drugs. What they need is to be understood, given different, more comfortable environments in the home and outside it, and they must be worked with via very different methods. It is not helpful for them to be ostracized by staff or other students in the school environment.

I remember one parent contacting me after she heard an interview I had given on this subject. She told me that she had taken her son off of the drugs that had been prescribed to settle his behavior. The child later told his mom that he finally felt like himself again, while on the drugs he felt out of touch with everything. He said that he could no longer feel himself when on the drugs. He had lost his inborn sentience. Fortunately he got it back.

Drugs are not the answer for the Children of Now. We cannot force them to fit into societal molds that were created based upon the implementation of archaic ideas. Drugs have a place in modern life; in certain cases they can be applied to bring comfort to a child who is off the charts overactive or anxious. But drugs are not for the convenience of adults so that they can manage children better. The rampant use of drugs in our world today is indicative of a much greater problem, which is lack of understanding and coping tools on the part of adults who work with children who have entirely different sensitivities and abilities in our fast-changing world. Instead, we as a society must revamp our social norms and mores to accept what is different and to bend in such a way that we can support these amazing children rather than forcing them into being something that is not natural for them. What can we do for them? We will discuss that in more detail in chapter 9.

CHAPTER 6

The Perfect Storm: How We Are Creating a Generation of Murderers and Sociopaths

Nearly every week we see in the news that a young person has committed a heinous act. Later we find out that there were problems in the home or signs or treatment of potential or diagnosed mental illness. We hear that everyone did the best they could . . .

I include these stories because they are part of the greater picture of the same evolutionary phenomenon. This much darker aspect of the journey of the Children of Now must be addressed as part of the greater whole. There are deep reasons for the types of disturbing situations we will discuss here.

I wish I could say that these cases are out of the ordinary, but they are not. Each is a sad indication of what can happen to the Children of Now or any child when families and society cannot or do not give them what they need. Don't get me wrong, I am not blaming anyone in particular for the stories I am using to make a point. What I am saying is that society as a whole is failing these kids. It truly does take a village.

Not knowing the kids in these cases personally it is impossible to say if they are Children of Now themselves, but they are part of the macro of this phenomenon so I feel it is vital to discuss their situations. What happens on subconscious levels is that the aggressors sense the difference of their victims and then attack.

Consider these examples and then we will explore the subject more deeply.

Dangers of Disaffection

At Virginia Tech in 2007 Seung-Hui Cho murdered thirty-three people and injured seventeen others. He was twenty-three years old when he opened fire on a busy campus and ultimately committed suicide by shooting himself in the head.

Cho wrote two stories as class assignments that spoke of sexual molestation and violence. The subject matter of these papers definitely warranted concern. It is understandable that an institution serving more than 25,000 year-round students can't monitor everything with every student. On the other hand, everything begins on a personal level. A student hands in his paper to someone, someone reads and grades it (hopefully), and gosh this didn't come to light until after it was too late?

Several days after the shooting, a package was delivered to a local news program with photos of Cho in various martial arts poses and brandishing various weapons. Apparently he had taken time between shootings to send it priority mail.

Dr. Michael Welner, one of those who reviewed the materials, believed that Cho's ranting offers little insight into the mental illness that may have triggered his rampage. He stated, "These videos do not help us understand Cho. They distort him. He was meek. He was quiet. This is a PR tape of him trying to turn himself into a Quentin Tarantino character." [1-8]

Seriously? How could they not see from the videos, school papers, and other propaganda materials this child had sent in just how terribly lacking confidence he was, and how he created an inner world that made him feel alive, invincible, and ultimately brought him to that fateful day.

Prior to coming to the United States from Korea, Cho had been diagnosed with selective mutism as well as a major depressive disorder. According to Wikipedia,

> Selective mutism (SM) is an anxiety disorder in which a person who is normally capable of speech does not speak in specific situations or to specific people. Selective mutism usually co-exists with shyness or social anxiety.

Sound familiar? This description fits a Transitional Child to a tee as someone who internalizes all sensitivities and emotions and evolves these into a fantasy world later acted out.

On March 21, 2013, De'Marquise Elkins tried to hold up a mother who had her baby boy in a stroller in Brunswick, Georgia. He told the mom that he wanted her money. She tried to tell him that she didn't have any, so he shot her in the leg. When Elkins tried to take her purse, she again said there was no money. Elkins then walked over to the stroller and shot the thirteen-month-old Antonio Santiago in the face, killing him. Elkins was found guilty of eleven counts, including two of felony murder and one of malice murder. [9]

In August of 2013, Christopher Lane was murdered just for the fun of it. He was visiting the Oklahoma town where his girlfriend lives. He was a budding baseball star, having come to the United States from Australia. He was a rising senior at East Central University in Ada, Oklahoma, a catcher who had started fourteen games and hit .250 for the Tigers the previous season. He was loved by everyone.

James Francis Edwards Jr., fifteen, and Chancey Allen Luna, sixteen, were charged with his first degree murder after he was shot and killed with a .22. A third teenager, Michael Dewayne Jones, seventeen, was charged as an accessory after the fact and with firing a weapon. All were charged as adults, according to the Stephens County District Attorney's Office.

On January 10, 2014, the *New York Daily News* reported that an eleven-year-old Dallas girl viciously stabbed a family member nine times while her victim slept one Saturday morning. Apparently the child was angry because the adult had pushed her into a couch and told her she wanted to give her away. The child waited for the family member to go to sleep and then viciously stabbed her nine times. The woman awoke and fought off the child and at this writing was in stable condition.

And I could cite hundreds more. *What on earth is going on?*

The Challenges of Modern Childhood

We have a sociological perfect storm of situations that may be challenging individually but put together harbor the potential for catastrophic events. While there are many fine families and parents in our world, there are events occurring that have changed the face of how we interact with our children. It takes a lot of energy to be a good parent, but with all of the mitigating factors now involved, it is nearly impossible for a parent to be 100 percent about a child no matter how good the intentions. Without meaning to, we have allowed too much power to be taken from parents and thrown our children to the wolves.

The new generation of children operates differently than previous generations. Their energy fields absorb the input of their surroundings and those in it even more quickly than their minds can process. Their frequencies are so high that they are deeply sensitive to the point they often can't tell what feelings are theirs and what feelings belong to someone else. This makes them extremely vulnerable to acting out, rebelling, or isolating. When children try to take on responsibility for everyone and everything around them, that is far too great a load to carry. The Children of Now want everything to be okay and will try to fix what feels broken. Or they will avoid what feels broken because they don't have a clue how to fix it. Most of us have enough trouble dealing with our own stuff!

Let's look at the factors coming together in this perfect storm bearing down on the lives and psyches of our children.

The Information Age

This era of information and expectation offers constant examples to our children of how they should act, what is "cool" or acceptable, what they should wear, what products they need, and well, you get the idea. Information streams live all of the time so that world events and local ones are continually blasting our kids with really mixed signals about how safe they are.

The adolescent is already experiencing a conundrum of feelings, emotions, and thoughts due to fluctuating and rising hormone levels and other internal changes. Add all of the incoming stimuli on top of that, and subconsciously the child may develop views of the world that are overwhelming.

In addition to the constant input children receive, add the Internet and available electronics such as cell phones and tablets. While these devices are great for education and convenient communication, they also tend to depersonalize the child's experience of others. Most communications have factored to texting, which is a language all its own. Words are truncated or cut down to just a few significant letters; whatever children need to know they can look up quickly without having to interact with anyone else. This robs them of the opportunity to be mentored and guided by the adults in this world. Children learn only impersonal facts without the accompanying emotion or experience-based guidance of the human interaction and therefore no basis of support for them.

On the TV show *Modern Family* there was recently an episode showing Phil, the dad, about to go out the front door. When he opened it, there stood Darrell, the airheaded boyfriend of his daughter Haley. Phil was startled at first, then said that he would call Haley for Darrell. Darrell told Phil that there was no need, they had already texted and Hayley would be down in a minute. It was a funny scene, but it was also a huge statement on the condition of our communication as well as how the family unit and normal expected social interactions have been replaced by technology. Parents are often circumvented, and no matter how much effort they put into monitoring their child's communications, it has become nearly impossible to keep up.

Social networking sites put additional pressure on kids. Children are forced to compare themselves and their experiences with others who post. Pictures and videos of parties, social events, comments about them, and even downright mean posts have become the norm. Comments show whether our children are respected (and respectful), what appears to be important to them, how others treat them, and a plethora of other important factors. While sometimes posts are simply made to impress or cajole, for the most part we can glean a micro version of a child's social life there.

Underlying the social networks is the same kind of pressure we used to get from our peers. The problem is that now it is all made public and available for the world to see. This adds deeply to the internal roiling of our children's self-worth.

Issues of Discipline

We have so many rules and regulations these days that many normal, well-intentioned parents are afraid to discipline their children particularly publically for fear of being ostracized, criticized, or getting in trouble with the law. On the flip side, if a child isn't disciplined, these days it is very likely that strangers will comment to the child's parents on their parenting skills.

For instance, my good friend who lives in a large city took her child to tryouts for toddler soccer. During the tryouts, her child threw a huge screaming tantrum because he wanted to play on his own terms. He went running across the different designated tryout areas, disrupting everything for everyone. He was hard to catch because he was flailing and screaming the entire time. My friend told me how embarrassing the whole thing was, and I made the comment that I would have let him have it for acting like that. She said that in her city if you spank your child in public or strongly discipline them you are at risk for child abuse charges. I was dumbfounded. When asked her more about it, she gave me several examples of how parents had been publically chastised or complaints filed by other well-meaning but extremely judgmental people. I have heard a number of stories in which parents are criticized openly for strongly disciplining their kids in public . . . or not.

Many parents feel that what their child does is a direct reflection of them as people. This perception can cause a parent to turn a blind eye or paralyze a well-meaning parent from acting on behalf of their child in order to avoid feeling inadequate.

Depending upon which source you read, the average amount of time parents spend directly with their children ranges from nineteen minutes per day to twelve hours a week. Whatever the case, how can we expect our children to develop in a fully connected way when they are in the hands of others or on their own most of the time? Many parents have to spend well over forty hours a week at work or work more than one job. Kids are left to fend for themselves or in the hands of other caregivers. Parents do not have enough time to develop a deeply bonded relationship with the kids. Instead, each member of the family tends to encapsulate, so we end up with a family unit made up of individuals carrying on isolated lives.

Bullying

Peer pressure is out of control, and bullying has become national news. It used to be that when a child acted like a bully he would be punished or made to experience what bullying feels like. Now, much of the bullying goes unnoticed until the target is in jeopardy emotionally or physically—if someone spots it at all. When a child is targeted by other kids, she is likely to internalize the problem, and that can result in feelings of insignificance or a shaded sense of self. The child begins to feel as if she is less than others in many ways, and as time goes on, those feelings turn into an ingrained belief. Since bullying is an embarrassment, children will not always seek out the assistance of adults. A strong child with good coping skills may be able to move past the situation, but these days, where can a child turn to learn those coping skills?

Consider these frightening statistics (emphasis is mine):

- Bully victims are between *two to nine times more likely* to consider suicide than kids who are not bullied, according to studies by Yale University.

- A study in Britain found that *at least half of suicides among young people* are related to bullying and ten- to fourteen-year-old girls may be at an even higher risk.

- According to statistics reported by *ABC News*, *nearly 30 percent of students are either bullies or victims of bullying*, and 160,000 kids stay home from school every day because of a fear of being bullied.

- Suicide is the *third primary cause of death among youngsters*, resulting in about 4,400 deaths per year, according to the CDC. For every suicide among young people, there are *at least 100 suicide attempts*. More than 14 percent of high school students have contemplated suicide, and nearly 7 percent have attempted it.

Child bullies have taken to social networking these days to get their points across. According to an article in *USA Today*, experts who have studied social aggression in teens, including bullying via the Internet, say such harassment is a widespread problem that has gained increased attention in the digital age, when written threats and taunts live indefinitely online. Bullying isn't limited to one aggressive child; it often becomes a group effort to belittle a target. About one-fifth of all teens report having experienced cyberbullying.

Children's desensitization by video games, movies, and other avenues of fantasy violence play a role in this. When children don't understand what dead is, they also can't understand what their cruelty does to the psyche of another child. When the method of transmitting mean messages is the same as for game-playing—as it is in cyberbullying—it dehumanizes the target even more.

Cases in point:

- According to CNN, twelve-year-old Rebecca Sedwick jumped from the top of an abandoned concrete plant after aggravated stalking on Facebook by as many as fifteen other girls bombarding her with messages such as "You should die" and "Why don't you go kill yourself?" Rebecca couldn't take it anymore. She changed one of her online screen names to "That Dead Girl" before climbing a tower at the plant and hurling herself to her death.

- Megan Taylor Meier (November 6, 1992–October 17, 2006), a teenager from Dardenne Prairie, Missouri, hanged herself three weeks before her fourteenth birthday. A year later, Meier's parents pushed for an investigation and her suicide was attributed to cyberbullying on MySpace.

The Children of Now are at much greater risk for bullying because they stand out as different. They are gentler, more aware, emotionally sensitive, and their increased sensitivities mean they have even less shielding than a normal child from the aggressive emotions of their peers.

Teen Suicides

We have seen a huge number of suicides among adolescents in the past several years.

Consider the extreme case of Maxwell Web, an autistic child from Independence, Kansas, who was found hanging in his family's garage and passed away the next day at an area hospital. Max had actually been diagnosed with "mental abuse by bullying." He also had had concerns that his behavior as an autistic child was annoying others and that they might have been complaining about him at school. Max even wrote a report about his autistic issues and handed it in, only to have it thrown away in front of him with the remark that no one was complaining. Max left his local school, but the damage was already done.

There is also the case of fifteen-year-old Dillan Custer who tried to kill himself after he was bullied at his high school in Ripley, Tennessee. Family members say the teen is one of the best students around. Several students at Ripley High School threatened to kill him. "Every child deals with this issue and it upsets me," said family friend Kelli Scallions. "It takes something this serious to bring awareness to the problem."

Because most schools are oversize, overpopulated, and often understaffed (or staff underpaid), our schools have become impersonalized. Teachers are pressured to follow the curriculum and rules of the school system but at the same time are overrun by too many students to be able to supervise the mental health and actions of them all. Because of this, both subtle and obvious changes can go unnoticed until it is too late.

Those who are really serious about suicide often don't speak about it directly. However, they may behave in certain ways that can tip you off. Some signs that a child is considering suicide are:

- Showing signs of depression (this might look like ongoing sadness), withdrawal from others, loss of interest in favorite activities, or difficulty sleeping or eating.

- Talking about or exhibiting an interest in death or dying.

- Engaging in dangerous or harmful activities that might include substance abuse or self-injury such as cutting.

- Disposing of or giving away favorite possessions and saying things to people that seem like a goodbye.

- Indicating that they just can't handle things anymore.

- Saying that things would be better without them.

If a child is exhibiting these symptoms or anything remotely similar, talk to them about your concerns and get them professional help right away from a counselor, a doctor, or at the emergency room if needed. It is better to take action even if you are uncertain of what is happening than to ignore these behaviors as a "phase they are going through."

There are times when it may not be obvious that a teen is thinking about suicide as in those following an intense episode of bullying. In a number of cases of suicide incited by bullying, the bullies had told the targets that they should kill themselves or that the world would be better without them. Anyone who overhears such statements should get help immediately for the target and bring to bear official attention on the bullies. Make an effort that instant to convince the victim that the bullies are wrong.

Other things that we can do to help prevent teen suicide:

- Take any and all talk, mentions, or threats of suicide seriously. Don't just tell the speaker that he or she is wrong or that there is a lot to live for; instead, *get immediate medical help.*

- Keep all weapons and medications of any kind away from someone at risk for suicide. Get these items *out of the house* or at least be sure they are securely locked up.

- Parents should support their teens to talk about any bullying that takes place. Bullying tends to escalate. Kids might feel embarrassed to admit they are the victims. Most kids don't want to own up to the fact that they have been bullied. Tell them that it's not their fault. Explain that they are being bullied and show them love and support. Get them professional help from the school, a counselor, the police, or a lawyer—*whatever it takes to remedy the situation fast*—if the bullying is serious.

- Parents must insist on being included in their children's friends lists on social networking sites so that they can spot if someone is posting mean messages about their child. Text messages are harder to keep up with, so parents should also consider checking their children's cell phones or tablets regularly.

- Parents who come across any serious bullying problem should *immediately* talk to school authorities about it and also arrange a meeting with the bully's parents.

- More states are enacting laws against bullying. If school authorities don't show satisfactory progress with an ongoing bullying issue, contact the police or your lawyer. In an acute situation, call law enforcement immediately.

- Anyone considering suicide should talk to someone right away or go to an emergency room. There are free suicide hotlines, such as 1-800-273-TALK (8255), out there. Suicide.com has a large number of resources available.

- Also important, if you are dealing with a family member or anyone else with thoughts of suicide or attempting suicide, make sure to get yourself some support. This can be from other family members, friends, at your church. Just make sure it is good, solid support. Also get your own professional help if needed.

Video Games

One of the most destructive aspects in society today is video games. While they can be challenging and fun, some of them have become so lifelike that our children are being desensitized to injury and death. They play games like Assassin's Creed, Call of Duty, and Halo, which place the kids in the middle of the action within a bloody war. Sure, they learn great hand-eye coordination, but at the same time they are learning that death isn't real, that if you die you get another life. They are learning that you get so many injuries before you die and during that process you have to kill or be killed. Are they just games? Not when the child spends hours and hours playing at the deficit of normal socialization. Instead of developing sympathy and empathy, the kids are learning that injuring and killing are fine because they can get another life if they lose that round.

For a mentally healthy well-adjusted child with great coping skills, moderate amounts of gaming can be okay. That is really up to the parent. But, for sensitive children who don't have a good sense of self, coping tools, or conflict resolution, they act like a match to dynamite.

Movies have become similar in their effect. Hollywood is fantastic in applying its creative forces to bring us into temporary all-encompassing fantasy worlds. But honestly, how many times can the hero of a movie walk through fire, get shot, crash a car, be beaten, stabbed, or worse without suffering any long-term detrimental effects?

With the computerization of special effects, everything on the screen seems so real. If a person were subjected even to the smallest amount of the abuse that we see in the movies in everyday life, that individual would be indefinitely incapacitated.

All of these issues combine to create the perfect storm of desensitization, depersonalization, warped social views, and a lack of normal conflict resolution that some children and young adults go on to embody in disturbing events in the real world. Put more than one similarly affected child together in a group, and we get a destructive gang mentality in which a dare to kill becomes just something to do and no regard whatsoever is given to the life that is snuffed out forever.

We *can* change all this. But doing so will require a huge alteration in how we live, love, work, and interact socially and within the family unit. Messages need to go out to the companies that thrive and profit immensely from selling examples of mayhem and killing that we can no longer accept these products in the name of healthy children and therefore the future of our society. This doesn't mean we need to take a puritanical perspective, but it does mean that we are responsible for what is happening in our world. We are the consumers; without our support these products would give way to others that perhaps would be more in the vein of healthfulness of our kids. There is nothing wrong with a great fantasy, but if we have to make things realistic, why not throw in some good old-fashioned genuineness and truth?

CHAPTER 7

GMOs, Our Environment, and Our Mutating World

There are factors that are affecting our Children of Now in ways that previous generations have never had to consider. While adults certainly experience these same problems, the Children of Now are exponentially influenced.

Foods are being genetically modified, and our environment is filled with pollutants, chemicals, drugs, and metals. All of that is entering the air around us, the foods we eat, the water we use. Everything that sustains our lives contains some sort of challenge.

When we ingest genetically modified foods, our system begins to adapt to the changes in ways that are not yet understood or admitted. When we absorb toxins through the air, our kin, or otherwise, they can wreak havoc on our systems as well. When we have high-frequency children as described earlier, they are far more susceptible. Because of that, not only are their physical bodies affected, their consciousness and its place in the third dimension are also impacted.

Though I am not an expert on these subjects, for the purpose of fostering an awareness of these issues I decided it was vital to include them in our discussion. The information herein is generally the result of my research on these topics.

GMOs

The genetic modification of our food sources is a subject of hot debate. When I was researching this chapter, it became quickly clear that the subject is a Pandora's box of information and opinions for and against, and it can be quite hard to know what is real or fanatic, responsibly written or simply comprised of opinions. This section offers a basic set of information on this issue, but I make no claim to be an expert on genetic engineering or genetically modified foods.

Is genetically altered food okay? Is it not okay? The answer depends upon whom you ask. In my research I came to the strong conclusion that genetically altered foods are doing some pretty terrible things to our bodies and our health. While genetic engineering covers territory such as cloning and other extremely interesting subjects, we will only be addressing what relates to our foods and in turn, the Children of Now and ourselves.

First of all, what exactly is a GMO?

A GMO (genetically modified organism) is the result of a laboratory process during which the genes from one species are harvested and then inserted into the gene of another species in an attempt to obtain a desired trait or characteristic. GMOs may also be known as transgenic organisms, genetic engineering (GE), or genetic modification (GM). No matter the name, the process is the same.

A genetically modified organism (GMO) is an organism whose genetic material has been altered. Those changes may include a mutation or a deletion or insertion of genes from another species to achieve characteristics that may be more desirable, such as larger size or resistance to diseases or bugs, water consumption and other end results. This term is usually applied to agricultural products interfered with for more control over cultivation. When a plant is changed in such ways, not only does its makeup change, how that makeup relates in our bodies changes too.

Genes are one of every living thing's most important parts. Since they make up our DNA, they can be compared to the motherboard in a computer. The motherboard is the brains to the entire machine. Without it, the machine is just an inert box of metal. Genes are also record keepers. They carry coding that has information about how we will look, our personalities, in fact, everything about us and how we relate to the world and internally as well.

Here are some basics on genes in general:

Every plant and animal is made of cells. In the center of each cell is the nucleus. Inside of the nucleus are strands of DNA. Within the DNA are shorter strands that are called genes.

Simply put, a gene is the basic physical and functional unit of heredity. They act as instructions to make molecules called proteins. You might call them our coding mechanism. Whatever is coded in the genes dictates what each gene instructs within our body. This can apply to how we look and our unique physical features.

In humans, genes can vary vastly in size from a few hundred DNA bases to more than two million. The Human Genome Project has estimated that humans have between twenty thousand and twenty-five thousand genes. Every person has two copies of each gene. One copy is inherited from each parent.

Genes work similarly in plants and animals. Each species has its own genes or coding that dictates what it is as well as its appearance and traits.

In genetic engineering DNA from one species is forced into the cells of another species, thus creating a transgenic organism—a living entity that has crossed species barriers and is now neither the original species nor the newly introduced one, but instead both combined—or at least their specific traits.

When it comes to our foods, genetic modification is carried out for many reasons. For instance in our food sources, genetic modification has made make plants less sensitive to herbicides, allowing farmers to spray for weeds without risk to the crops.

The Non GMO Shopping Site (www.nongmoshoppingguide.com) lists other interesting examples of GM:

- Spider genes were inserted into goat DNA, in an attempt to achieve goat milk that would contain spiderweb proteins for use in bulletproof vests.

- Cow genes turned pigskins into cowhides.

- Jellyfish genes lit up pigs' noses in the dark.

- Arctic fish genes gave tomatoes and strawberries tolerance to frost.

- Potatoes were modified to glow in the dark when they needed watering.

- Human genes were inserted into corn to produce spermicide.

- Corn has been engineered with human genes (Dow).

- Sugarcane has been engineered with human genes (Hawaii Agriculture Research Center).

- Corn has been engineered with jellyfish genes (Stanford University).

- Tobacco has been engineered with lettuce genes (University of Hawaii).

- Rice has been engineered with human genes (Applied Phytologics).

- Corn has been engineered with hepatitis virus genes (Prodigene).

Some of the problems that scientists have found during genetic engineering are unintended side effects. For instance, plants create toxins; they weather differently and may contain too many or too few nutrients. They may become diseased, malfunction, or even die. When foreign genes are inserted into a host, this creates a different set of instructions in what would have otherwise been the plant's "norm." Because of this, dormant genes may be inadvertently activated or the overall functioning of the genes altered. New or unknown proteins may be created or the input and output of existing proteins may be altered.

Proteins are generally the basis of our DNA system and therefore communications within our bodies.

The effects of consuming these new combinations of proteins are unknown.

Many GM foods have antibiotic-resistant genes because, since there is a low success rate in genetic modification, scientists have created marker genes so that they can track which genes are actually picking up the genetically introduced traits. These marker genes are resistant to the types of antibiotics generally used for humans and animals.

As species are altered, the entire food chain is too. For instance, plants grow and humans, insects, and animals eat them. As we take in plants that are no longer what they once were, our bodies process them differently. The new, modified proteins may cause our bodies to produce new or different proteins that require our bodies to act or react differently, not only to foods but in their everyday functioning. This can cause autoimmune issues, as we begin to physiologically change to adapt or we don't. In either case, these new items in our bodies are not natural or part of our internal norm, so our bodies begin to try to rid themselves of the invading species. As that occurs, the autoimmune system is triggered over and over again, and we begin to suffer from allergies, digestive issues, or worse.

Decayed or dying plants may get into our waterways and be eaten by aquatic life, which then may be eaten by other animals. We are at risk for molecular changes based upon genetically altered foods entering into our systems via such indirect routes. As our bodies must learn to process genetically modified foods, we are also at risk of unknown symptoms or long-term effects that may be detrimental to our health.

The American Academy of Environmental Medicine (AAEM) recently released its position paper on genetically modified foods stating that "GM foods pose a serious health risk" and calling for a cessation to the production of GM foods.

Citing several animal studies, the AAEM concludes that "there is more than a casual association between GM foods and adverse health effects" and that "GM foods pose a serious health risk in the areas of toxicology, allergy and immune function, reproductive health, and metabolic, physiologic and genetic health."

The AAEM has further called for a moratorium on GM food, with the implementation of immediate long-term safety testing and labeling of GM food. They have recommended that physicians educate their patients, the medical community, and the public to avoid GM foods. They have also requested them to consider the role of GM foods in their patients' disease processes. The AAEM is just one of many organizations worldwide calling for these steps to be taken.

Globally only one-tenth of the world's cropland supports GM plants. Four countries—the United States, Canada, Brazil, and Argentina—grow 90 percent of the planet's GM crops. GM crops are banned in eighty countries or require labeling; the United States and Canada are not among them. Europe has shown a greater aversion for GMOs due to more balanced reporting in their press on the health and environmental dangers. In Europe, at least

174 regions and more than 4,500 councils and local governments have declared themselves GM free.

So what foods are genetically modified? Presently commercialized GM crops in the United States include soy (94 percent), cotton (90 percent), canola (90 percent), sugar beets (95 percent), corn (88 percent), Hawaiian papaya (more than 50 percent), zucchini and yellow squash (over 24,000 acres).

Other potential sources of GMO may be somewhat secondary but can certainly have the same effects as a direct-source GMO. Listed below are other products and those derived from the list above, including oils, soy protein, soy lecithin, cornstarch, corn syrup, and high fructose corn syrup.

- Meat, eggs, and dairy products from animals that have eaten GM feed (and the majority of the GM corn and soy is used for feed)

- Dairy products from cows injected with rbGH (a GM hormone)

- Food additives, enzymes, flavorings, and processing agents, including the sweetener aspartame (NutraSweet®) and rennet used to make hard cheeses (Pharmaceutical companies use aspartame in some laxatives, supplements, and children's vitamins.)

- Honey and bee pollen that may have GM sources of pollen

- Nonfood items including cosmetics, soaps, detergents, shampoo, and bubble bath

The Gluten Issue

Gluten seems to be a new buzzword when it comes to diets, allergies, weight gain, and other physical issues. But concern about gluten is not a fad, it is a serious problem.

One of the things we hear a lot about is gluten intolerance. What does that mean? Why is it an important subject relative to the Children of Now? To find that out we must look at gliadin. What is gliadin? According to Wikipedia,

Gliadin is a class of proteins present in wheat and several other cereals within the grass genus *Triticum*. Gliadins and gluten are essential for giving bread the ability to rise properly during baking. Gliadins and glutenins are the two main components of the gluten fraction of the wheat seed. This gluten is found in products such as wheat. Gluten is split about evenly between the gliadins and glutenins although there are variations found in different sources. Gliadin is the soluble aspect of it, while glutenin is insoluble. There are three main types of gliadin (α, γ and ω) to which the body is intolerant in coeliac (or celiac) disease.

According to the January 6, 2014 issue of *First for Women*, cardiologist William Davis said that when a certain protein was changed in the grain to make it more bug resistant, it caused changes in the cellular level of plants. According to Davis, hundreds of studies have shown that the gliadin of 2013 is more inflammatory in the body and more likely to trigger the autoimmune process than the gliadin of 1960. This effect has caused a staggering increase in the incidence of gluten intolerance over the past fifty years.

This protein also stimulates appetite by invigorating the opiate receptors in the brain, making people specifically crave carbohydrates to the point that the typical person who eats wheat actually consumes between 440 and 800 additional calories per day. Consequently, there is a huge number of overweight kids. This issue also increases instances of diabetes.

When genetically modified, the altered wheat contains a "sugar-starch" (amylopectin) that raises blood sugar higher than older forms of grain. Scientists at the University of Sydney in Australia found that two slices of whole wheat bread can produce a more pronounced blood sugar spike than six tablespoons of pure table sugar. As a result, eating wheat (bread, cereal, pasta, etc.) is often followed by a blood-sugar crash three hours later that causes fatigue, mental fog, and irritability.

In the October 28, 2013 issue of *Woman's World* magazine, the cover story was "Gene Lee Nolin's Thyroid Cure!" on how the actress lost fifty pounds. She was one of the *Baywatch* hotties in the 1990s TV series. The article shared a number of important bits on the gluten/gliadin subject. In it, Mary Shoman, author of *Thyroid Diet Revolution*, is quoted as saying the "thyroid produces hormones that allow the body to turn food and stored fat into energy. It is the master gland of metabolism. Yet despite its powerful role, it is quite vulnerable."

According to the article, research suggests that as many as ninety-eight million of us will develop thyroid issues at some point in our lives. Fortunately, one major thyroid offender is gluten, and we can eliminate that from our diets. Shoman states, "Gluten is a sticky wheat protein so similar in shape to thyroid hormone that it can enter and block the body's receptors for thyroid hormone." So though we may produce these hormones naturally, our bodies aren't able to use them properly. They can't plug in.

Later in the article, David Brownstein, MD, and author of *Overcoming Thyroid Disorders*, states that, "In the last 30 years, wheat has been genetically modified to have a higher gluten content. So many more people are having trouble, and more and more doctors are recommending a gluten-free approach to people with thyroid or weight issues."

Sara Gottfried, MD, author of *The Hormone Cure*, recommends replacing white carbs (bread, sugar, pasta) with sweet potatoes, brown rice, and beans, adding that even some supposedly gluten-free foods can spike blood sugar, causing inflammation in the body and dampening thyroid function.

The bottom line is this modified gluten is causing weight gain and possible diabetes as well as thyroid dysfunction in a huge percentage of our population, including our kids.

According to a wonderful and informative blog by Wellness Mama (*wellnessmama.com/3684/is-soy-healthy/*), soy is another mean culprit in our ill-health and development. She lists the following reasons that soy is harmful to our health:

- Soybeans have phytoestrogens that imitate the body's natural estrogen hormones. In men, this can lead to a testosterone imbalance, infertility, low sperm count, and even an increased possibility of cancers. In women, soy can cause estrogen dominance, which has been linked to infertility, menstrual problems, and cancer.

- These phytoestrogens are so potent that a baby eating only soy formula is consuming the *same amount* of hormones as in four birth control pills per day.

- The high levels of phytic acid in soy interfere with the body's ability to absorb important minerals such as zinc, calcium, copper, iron, and magnesium (which many people are dangerously lacking in already).

- Soy also has protease inhibitors that can actually block the enzymes that are needed for the digestion of certain proteins.

- The goitrogens in soy are strong antithyroid compounds that can lead to endocrine disruption and thyroid problems. Infants on soy formula have a much greater risk of autoimmune thyroid disease. Cooking does not remove goitrogens.

- Soy is often recommended as an alternate food for celiac and gluten-intolerant people, but its lectins can be destructive to the intestines and can also prevent healing even when gluten is removed.

- Eating soy foods intensifies the body's need for Vitamin D, Vitamin B-12, calcium, and magnesium. Many people are already deficient in these vitamins and minerals even before eating soy.

Almost all soybeans grown today are genetically modified and "Roundup ready." They contain a gene that overrules the effect of weed killers on the soy plants. In other words, they can be sprayed with lethal weed killer but not be affected. There is some evidence that this gene can mutate and create a pesticide-like toxin in the body. Soybeans also strip the soil of nutrients, leaving it depleted.

Animals fed soy can experience many of the health consequences that people suffer as a result of eating the modified soy. Those harmful properties are then passed on in their meat, milk, and *basically anything we use from the animals.*

Sadly, how often do well-meaning people substitute soy as an alternative to gluten or other foods that can be harmful?

Most parents believe that they are giving their children a healthy breakfast of cereal, but that may be far from the truth. Then, we send them off to school with sandwiches made out of whole grain bread, not realizing that one slice of that bread can have as much impact on their blood sugar as six tablespoons of sugar. School cafeterias very often serve pizzas, hamburgers, or hot dogs on buns, again bad grain. Corn is one of the worst modified foods. And high fructose corn syrup is in everything from ketchup to yogurt to fruit juices to cereals, breads, soft drinks, and so many other products.

All of these frightening things can affect even the most "normal" child. With their high-frequency energy systems, the Children of Now are even more susceptible. Energetically, the digestive tract is the densest of all in our physical systems. In a high-frequency system, the digestive tract is the first to degrade energetically. Not only does digestion and absorption of our nutrients take place within the intestinal tract, our autoimmune system lives there too.

When we introduce altered genetics in the form of foods or other products into our bodies, our bodies do not fully recognize the altered products as normal or natural, and so the natural response of our system is to begin fighting the foreign materials. Then there is the thyroid issue with cell receptors being plugged with the wrong stuff, and the sugar issues. Suddenly we have a population of thyroid-deficient, overweight children who suffer from inflammation and histamine reactions. Even worse, many of these kids have a greater possibility of being diabetic later in life.

Outside of the "normal" terrible effects of GMOs most of us face, autistic children are particularly sensitive to the environment and foods. These high-frequency kids are often physically devastated by the affects of GMOs and toxins in our environment. I found a great article on this subject that ran in *Medical News Today*:

Autism Linked To Industrial Food Or Environment
Monday 16 April 2012 - 1pm PST
Written By Petra Rattue

A new study in Clinical Epigenetics, suggests that the epidemic of **autism** amongst children in the U.S. may be associated with the typical American diet. The study by Renee Dufault and his team explores how mineral deficiencies, affected by dietary factors, such as high fructose corn syrup (HFCS), could have a potential impact on how the human body frees itself of common toxic chemicals, for instance, pesticides and mercury.

The release comes shortly after the Centers for Disease Control and Prevention (CDC) issued a report that estimates a 78% increase in **autism** spectrum disorder (ASD) between 2002 and 2008 amongst eight year olds. At present, 1 in 88 children has ASD, with the rate being almost five times higher in boys than girls.

Dr. David Wallinga, a physician at the Institute for Agriculture and Trade Policy (IATP) and co-author of the study, said:

"To better address the explosion of autism, it's critical we consider how unhealthy diets interfere with the body's ability to eliminate toxic chemicals, and ultimately our risk for developing long-term health problems like autism."

Leading author, Commander (ret.) Renee Dufault (U.S. Public Health Service), a former Food and Drug Administration (FDA) toxicologist, developed an innovative scientific approach called "macroepigenetics", which describes the subtle side effects of HFCS consumption, as well as other dietary factors on the human body and their relationship with chronic disorders. By using the model, researchers can take nutritional and environmental factors as well as genetic makeup into account and observe how these interact and contribute to potential developments of a certain health outcome.

Dufault, who is also a licensed special education teacher and founder of the Food Ingredient and Health Research Institute (FIHRI) remarks:

*"With autism rates skyrocketing, our public educational system is under extreme **stress**."*

The authors also discovered, as part of the current study, that the number of autistic children who receive special educational services in the U.S. has risen by 91% between 2005 and 2010.

Given that autism and related disorders affect brain development, the researchers decided to establish how environmental and dietary factors, such as HFCS consumption, could together contribute to the disorder. For instance, consuming HFCS is associated with the dietary loss of zinc. Zinc insufficiency has a negative impact on the body's ability to eliminate heavy metals. Several heavy metals, including arsenic, cadmium and mercury are potent toxins that have adverse effects on young children's brain development.

Other beneficial minerals, like **calcium**, are also affected by HFCS consumption, as a loss of calcium further aggravates the devastating impact of exposure to lead on fetuses and children's brain development. Insufficient calcium levels can also debilitate the body's ability of getting rid of organophosphates, which belong to a class of pesticides that the EPA, as well as independent scientists have long ago recognized as having especially toxic affects on the young developing brain.

Dr. Richard Deth, a professor of Pharmacology at Northeastern University and a co-author of the study explained:

> "Rather than being independent sources of risk, factors like **nutrition** and exposure to toxic chemicals are cumulative and synergistic in their potential to disrupt normal development. These epigenetic effects can also be transmitted across generations. As autism rates continue to climb it is imperative to incorporate this new epigenetic perspective into prevention, diagnosis and treatment strategies."

How and why children develop autism is a complex issue that is influenced by numerous different factors. This study has provided an insight into the comprehensive interaction between several of the factors that could lead to the development of this debilitating neurodevelopment disorder. However, in order to control the autism epidemic within the U.S., researchers must continue to analyze the affects of industrialized food systems and exposure to environmental toxins on

ASD. These factors are of crucial importance and further research must focus on these key areas to gain further insight.

Recently several states included referendums on their dockets to require labeling of GMO foods. For the most part, these issues were defeated due to the lobbying by large corporations, which sent out propaganda prior to the election about why that labeling was a bad idea. We really must wake up on this subject and demand healthy food production that does not contain altered genetics, chemicals, or other harmful ingredients. The really sad thing is we as a general public are ignorant of just how badly we are being poisoned on a day-to-day basis by companies that make their bottom lines more important than the people who buy their products.

Our finely tuned children will suffer the worst. Their parents struggle hourly most days trying to do what is right, but the situation has become untenable. Regulations have been put in place that are deceptive, such that the meaning of "organic" can vary when it applies to foods imported from other countries and even within the United States. Soon we will be forced to consider options for going back to homegrown foods, but then again, most of the seeds that are available on the open market are also genetically altered. To avoid them, look for heirloom seeds, which are not genetically modified.

Environmental Factors

Our foods are not the only contributing factor to autism and other behavioral issues in our children. Our environment contains chemicals, viruses, bacteria, and other factors that maybe altering our brains and how our immune systems work.

According to *Scientific American*, a new study led by Irva Hertz-Picciotto, an epidemiology professor at the University of California, has recently related autism and the environment. The scientists who authored the report encourage a nationwide shift in autism research to identify and focus on likely elements in the environment that babies and fetuses are exposed to including pesticides, viruses, and chemicals in household products.

"It's time to start looking for the environmental culprits responsible for the remarkable increase in the rate of autism in California," says Hertz-Picciotto.

Many chemicals in the environment are neurodevelopmental toxins, which means they change how the brain grows. Mercury, polychlorinated biphenyls, lead, brominated flame retardants, and pesticides are good examples. While exposure to some questionable substances—such as PCBs—has declined in recent decades, for others—including flame retardants used in furniture and electronics and pyrethroid insecticides—it has increased.

One study not yet published suggests that mothers of autistic children were twice as prone to use pet flea shampoos, which contain organophosphates or pyrethroids. Another new study has found an association between autism and phthalates, which are compounds used in vinyl and cosmetics. Additional household products such as antibacterial soaps could also have ingredients that damage the brain by changing the immune system, Hertz-Picciotto says.

In addition to ongoing factors in the environment that hurt our children, fetuses and infants may be exposed to a comparatively new infectious microbe, such as a virus or bacteria that could be altering the immune system or even brain structure. A good example of this occurred in the 1970s, when autism rates increased due to the rubella virus.

The exact cause of changing immune and brain systems may ultimately be discovered in the microbial and chemical arenas, or it may be found to be a compound of factors that alone pose no risk but combined change the literal functioning and construct of human brains or immune and other systems.

The National Autism Association says that the theory that parental practices are responsible for autism has long been disproven. While mainstream science discounts vaccinations as a cause, members of the association feel that they are responsible for generating autism in a subset of kids and that an overly aggressive vaccination schedule coupled with toxic adjuvants in the vaccines could affect persons who have a family history of autoimmune disorders specifically. There are many stories that describe a healthy baby or toddler having drastic reactions after receiving vaccines. What was once a normal child all of a sudden changes. Seizures are also noted as a result of vaccines. I have heard this from a number of parents and have witnessed this firsthand.

Adverse events can and do happen, as with any medication; vaccinations are no exception. Research to investigate and reduce adverse reactions in immunized people is currently nonexistent. The National Autism Association believes that:

- Vaccinations can trigger or exacerbate autism in some, if not many, children, particularly those who are genetically predisposed to immune, autoimmune, or inflammatory conditions.

- Other environmental exposures may set off or worsen autism in certain children, particularly those who are genetically predisposed to immune, autoimmune, or inflammatory conditions.

According to the National Autism Association, mainstream research has identified other contributing factors for autism:

- Scientists think that exposure to the chemicals in pesticides may adversely affect those who are genetically predisposed to autism, leading them to develop the full-blown disorder.

- A study found that age when pregnant may be a factor. Women who are forty years old have a 50 percent greater risk of having a child with autism than women who are between twenty and twenty-nine years old.

- Babies that have been exposed to certain pharmaceuticals in utero, including SSRIs, valproic acid, and thalidomide, have been found to have a higher risk of autism.

- A study found that children born to mothers who live within 1,000 feet of freeways have two times the risk of autism.

- One study found that women who recounted not taking prenatal vitamins immediately before and during a pregnancy were twice as likely to have a child with autism.

Not to be excluded when discussing environmental issues are secondhand drugs that find their way into our water systems as well as into the food chain after they are eliminated by the patient. This includes drugs administered to domesticated animals and all drugs taken by human beings. With the push by big pharma to have us take more drugs by encouraging us in advertisements to tell our doctors what we want, more and more people believe that they need a prescription. Once the drugs are in our bodies, what isn't used gets eliminated. Think about it: Antidepressants, antipsychotics, thyroid medication (on the rise since so many people have thyroid issues due to GMOs), arthritis drugs, and heart medication all seeping into our environment and therefore our food chain.

Also, we do not yet know the long-term effects of the drugs that are given to livestock and other food source animals that are eliminated onto the ground then washed into the earth and waterways and their combinations on the overall food chain. The possibility exists for mutations and adaptations in our chemical makeup that can and likely will affect our bodies and minds as a result of this type of pollution.

There are any numbers of factors that may contribute to autism generally and that particularly affect our Children of Now. Environmental research holds the key to unlocking the mysteries of the autism epidemic. What we don't know is how our children in general are to be affected over the long term by these hidden dangers.

As with any important life-affecting subject, it is advisable and important that you do your own research.

If you want to check the safety of your child's vaccines, you can go to the National Vaccine Information Center (www.nvic.org) for assistance.

CHAPTER 8

Vaccines

He was developing normally when he was 18 months old then he suddenly started regressing. His speech slowed and stopped completely, he started acting like a baby again. But he also seems very intelligent. Some doctors have suggested autism, but they are not sure because some days he seems ok and others he just "disappears" into his own world. The doctors are astounded because he seems so bright. He can do puzzles that 6 year olds can't do and is very good with technology. He stares at me and I can feel he is trying to tele-pathically say something but I simply can't get it. I wish I knew what was going through his mind . . .
—Mother of a Child of Now

I can't tell you how many times I have heard different versions of this scenario. This exact one often plays out very soon if not immediately after vaccines are administered. It seems that the vaccines may have a cumulative effect that comes to a head right around eighteen months and sometimes not until twenty-four months. It can also happen earlier, right after the first or second vaccine shots.

The vaccine issue seems to relate mostly to the autism epidemic, but it can apply to all of our high-frequency kids.

They are extremely sensitive, particularly when other factors predispose them in addition to an affected energy field.

Vaccines can do a world of good and have helped to eradicate some pretty nasty diseases. On the other hand, there may be underlying factors that traditional medicine does not consider such as our subtle energy fields.

Often when there is an injury or surgery, the energy field can be damaged or pushed out of harmony as a whole or partially. Though not fully understood or accepted by some, energy work makes a powerful contribution to treating the physical body. When the energy field has been affected, it is an intangible issue that influences the physical in powerful ways, sometimes even keeping healing from happening as it should. Utilizing energetic healing techniques goes a long way toward the speed and fullness of healing. Reiki, Healing Touch, or especially Touching the Light treatments in conjunction with, during, or after surgery assist patients in healing faster and with fewer complications. Using these techniques assists in normalizing the energy field.

Since we all consist of a complex system of energy and other etheric aspects, there are a multitude of areas that can be affected that medical testing may not currently detect. This is a sad state of affairs since such considerations could go a long way in alleviating many of the problems we are seeing in our Children of Now, particularly in the arena of autism.

According to the CDC, vaccines are perfectly safe. An article on their website says that:

A new study evaluating parents' concerns of "too many vaccines too soon" and autism has been published online in the Journal of Pediatrics *(http://jpeds.com/webfiles/images/journals/ympd/JPEDSDeStefano.pdf) March 29, 2013. It adds to the conclusion of a 2004 (http://www.iom.edu/reports/2004/immunization-safety-review-vaccines-and-autism.aspx) (http://www.cdc.gov/Other/disclaimer.html) comprehensive review by the Institute of Medicine (IOM) that there is not a causal relationship between certain vaccine types and autism. The results provide relevant data for the current childhood immunization schedule.*

The study looked at the amount of antigens from vaccines received on one day of vaccination and the amount of antigens from vaccines received in total during the first two years of life and found no connection to the development of autism spectrum disorder (ASD) in children. Antigens are substances in vaccines that cause the body's immune system to produce antibodies to fight disease.

Researchers collected data from 3 managed care organizations in a group of 256 children with ASD compared with 752 children without ASD.

The study's main findings report:

1. The total amount of antigens from vaccines received was the same between children with ASD and those that did not have ASD.

2. Children with ASD with regression (the loss of developmental skills during the second year of life) did not receive an increased number of vaccine antigens when compared to children without ASD with regression.

3. *The number of vaccine antigens has decreased in recent years. Although the routine childhood vaccine immunization schedule in 2013 contains more vaccines than the schedule in the late 1990s, the maximum number of vaccine antigens that a child would be exposed to by 2 years of age in 2013 is 315, compared with several thousand in the late 1990s. This is due to changes in the vaccines. For example, the older whole cell pertussis vaccine causes the body to produce about 3,000 different antibodies, whereas the newer acellular pertussis vaccines cause the production of 6 or fewer different antibodies.*

An infant's immune system is capable of responding to a large amount of immunologic stimuli and, from time of birth, infants are exposed to hundreds of viruses and countless antigens that are not associated with vaccination. This study demonstrates that autism spectrum disorder is not associated with immunological stimulation from vaccines during the first 2 years of life.

Parents should expect the vaccines their children receive are safe and effective. CDC, along with other federal agencies, is committed to assuring the safety of vaccines through rigorous pre-licensure trials and post-licensure monitoring.

So there you have it, the official word from the powers that be. No harm, no foul. Or is there?

Having heard variations on the quote at the beginning of this chapter so many times, it is impossible for me to ignore the fact that something else may be going on. Not only are there stories like this, there are many others concerning normal children having seizure activity after they receive their vaccines.

Our energy system is electromagnetic in nature and so is our consciousness. A fantastic illustrated full discussion of the nature of consciousness and how it works can be found in my book *The Secret History of Consciousness*. Consciousness is not bound to any space or time. It is faster than the speed of light and works in conjunction with our DNA. Our DNA encodes how we look and how our bodies work and respond and a gazillion other things. The higher our state of consciousness, the more active our DNA becomes, and the energy field of the DNA grows larger. Our DNA can be and is modified and influenced by our environment. We can also experience changes from our environment that do not originate with our DNA but are caused by other influences. This is called epigenetics.

In biology, and specifically genetics, epigenetics is the study of heritable changes in gene activity that are *not* caused by changes in the DNA sequence. The term can also be used to describe the study of stable, long-term changes in the transcriptional potential of a cell that are not necessarily heritable. Unlike in simple genetics based on changes to the DNA sequence (the genotype), the changes in gene expression or cellular phenotype of epigenetics have other causes, such as environmental influences.

Put simply, we can experience physical changes that we haven't inherited, but that have been caused by factors around us. These influences can result in the expression of different genes that are encoded in our DNA. The result of this can come in the form of dysfunction or even deformity. In epigenetics, environmental influencers cause changes that turn good genes and bad genes on and off, and depending on the changes in the genes, our bodies may begin to act or respond differently. Those changes can then become hereditary.

Due to the sensitivity of our new children, we must be diligent about what is allowed to affect our environment. Toxins in our environment will impact our children first since they are in the developmental stages of their lives.

Our light fields, which are comprised of many levels of frequencies and harmonics and in total express our vital energy, are currently measurable. Changes to DNA are also measurable. DNA is not only coded, it is intelligent. If it is given instructions or receives other information as from the composition of toxins in our environment, our DNA will respond by changing to fit those instructions, even if they aren't good for us. Our DNA is on duty all of the time, doing its best to keep us healthy and balanced, but when it receives instructions from our environment, it will adapt accordingly even if that means the adaptation is detrimental to our health.

Here is one example of how our DNA responds to what is happening around us. If you have a sample of DNA in one place and then another identical sample another place far away, if you create an effect on one strand, the far distant one will respond exactly the same. This has been proven in the lab. And this perfectly describes not only how our consciousness works, but how easily influenced our DNA can be by other factors.

Further, since the Children of Now generally operate at a higher frequency, their refined energy fields are already working in tandem with expanded DNA fields *as consciousness*, so anything that upsets that fine balance can send a child into a tailspin of not so good effects. *So when the DNA is affected so is the functioning of consciousness as it applies in our physical world.* Vaccines and other things can do that and so can environmental issues.

Remember the images from Figures 2–6 earlier in the book? They illustrate what can happen in a child's energy field when vaccines and the ingredients in those vaccines even subtly change the energy field by expanding it.

A child with somewhat lower frequencies (this has nothing at all to do with whether a child is normal or not or their abilities in general—remember, everyone has a different harmonic arrangement!) will adapt more easily to vaccines than a higher-frequency Child of Now. Certain ingredients in the vaccines may cause the energy field to expand or move or change in different ways. Sometimes those changes do not normalize over time, and instead, the field stays dysfunctional. When it does, we begin to see changes in the child just like the mom in the quote described or worse. Some children hit the dirt and become clearly dysfunctional in a more profound way. The extent varies from child to child depending upon how their harmonics responded in the first place.

There is a huge battle going on about whether or not vaccines are okay for kids. The opinions are much like opposite poles. Too many kids have exhibited symptoms for us to ignore what is going on. The problem is that modern medicine does not consider the subtle energy field when testing or researching the effects of any drug or vaccine. The reason they come up with perfectly normal outcomes is that they are only measuring biology. The energy field is barely acknowledged, let alone considered or tested. But the vaccine question has been studied extensively, and there are other reports that suggest that vaccines are more than not okay. A great deal of information has been discovered, but the studies are hit-and-miss. While the information is good, we still don't have the whole story.

There is a great list of studies published by collective-evolution.com that provides an example of how efforts to prove vaccines contribute to or cause autism are all over the place. Each study is disturbing in its implications on its own, but in trying to make sense of the total picture, the average person gets lost in the forest pretty fast.

Here is an excerpt from the web article citing twenty-two different studies that have found evidence that vaccines are in fact contributing to the autism epidemic. While the studies may focus on different issues, they indicate a need for extreme care and diligence on our parts and the parts of our children:

• A study published in the journal *Annals of Epidemiology* (*http://www.ncbi.nlm.nih.gov/pubmed/11895129*) has shown that giving the Hepatitis B vaccine to newborn baby boys could triple the risk of developing an autism spectrum disorder compared to boys who were not vaccinated as neonates. The research was conducted at Stony Brook University Medical Centre, NY.

• A study published in the *Journal of Inorganic Biochemistry* (*http://omsj.org/reports/tomljenovic%202011.pdf*) by researchers at the Neural Dynamics Group, Department of Ophthalmology and Visual Sciences at the University of British Columbia determined that Aluminum, a highly neurotoxic metal and the most commonly used vaccine adjuvant may be a significant contributing factor to the rising prevalence of ASD in the Western World. They showed that the correlation between ASD prevalence and the Aluminum adjuvant exposure appears to be the highest at 3-4 months of age. The studies also show that children from countries with the highest ASD appear to have a much higher exposure to Aluminum from vaccines. The study points out that several prominent milestones of brain development coincide with major vaccination periods for infants. These include the onset of synaptogenesis (birth), maximal growth velocity of the hippocampus and the onset of amygdala maturation. Furthermore, major developmental transition in many bio-behavioral symptoms such as sleep, temperature regulation, respiration and brain wave patterns, all of which are regulated by the neuroendocrine network. Many of these aspects of brain function are known to be impaired in autism, such as sleeping and brain wave patterns.

• According to the FDA, vaccines represent a special category of drugs as they are generally given to healthy individuals. Further according to the FDA, "this places significant emphasis on their vaccine safety". While the FDA does set an upper limit for Aluminum in vaccines at no more that 850/mg/dose, it is important to note that this amount was selected empirically from data showing that Aluminum in such amounts enhanced the antigenicity of the vaccine, rather than from existing safety. Given that the scientific evidence appears to indicate that vaccine safety is not as firmly established as often believed, it would seem ill advised to exclude pediatric vaccinations as a possible cause of adverse long-term neurodevelopment outcomes, including those associated with autism.

• A study published in the *Journal of Toxicology and Environmental Health, Part A: Current Issues (http://www.ncbi.nlm. nih.gov/pubmed/21623535)* by the Department of Economics and Finance at the University of New York shows how researchers suspect one or more environmental triggers are needed to develop autism, regardless of whether individuals have a genetic predisposition or not. They determined that one of those triggers might be the "battery of vaccinations that young children receive." Researchers found a positive and statistically significant relationship between autism and vaccinations. They determined that the higher the proportion of children receiving recommended vaccinations, the higher the prevalence of autism. A 1percent increase in vaccination was associated with an additional 680 children having autism. The results suggest that vaccines may be linked to autism and encourages more in depth study before continually administering these vaccines.

• A study published in the *Journal of Toxicology* (*http://www.hindawi.com/journals/jt/2013/801517/*) by the Department of Neurosurgery at the Methodist Neurological Institute in Houston has shown that ASD is a disorder caused by a problem in brain development. They looked at B cells and their sensitivity levels to thimerosal, a commonly used additive in many vaccines. They determined that ASD patients have a heightened sensitivity to thimerosal, which would restrict cell proliferation that is typically found after vaccination. The research shows that individuals who have this hypersensitivity to thimerosal could make them highly susceptible to toxins like thimerosal, and that individuals with a mild mitochondrial defect may be affected by thimerosal. The fact that ASD patients' B cells exhibit hypersensitivity to thimerosal tells us something.

• A study published in the *Journal of Biomedical Sciences* (*http://www.ncbi.nlm.nih.gov/pubmed/12145534*) determined that the autoimmunity to the central nervous system may play a causal role in autism. Researchers discovered that because many autistic children harbor elevated levels of measles antibodies, they should conduct a serological study of measles-mumps-rubella (MMR) and myelin basic protein

(MBP) autoantibodies. They used serum samples of 125 autistic children and 92 controlled children. Their analysis showed a significant increase in the level of MMR antibodies in autistic children. The study concludes that the autistic children had an inappropriate or abnormal antibody response to MMR. The study determined that autism could be a result from an atypical measles infection that produces neurological symptoms in some children. The source of this virus could be a variant of MV, or it could be the MMR vaccine.

• A study published in the *Annals of Clinical Psychiatry* suggests that autism is likely triggered by a virus, and that measles virus (MV and/or MMR vaccine) might be a very good candidate. It supports the hypothesis that a virus-induced autoimmune response may play a causal role in autism.

• A study published in the *American Journal of Clinical Nutrition* (*http://ajcn.nutrition.org/content/80/6/1611.full*) determined that an increased vulnerability to oxidative stress and decreased capacity for methylation may contribute to the development and clinical manifestation of autism. It's well known that viral infections cause increased oxidative stress. Research suggests that metals, including those found in many vaccines are directly involved in increasing oxidative stress.

• A study published by the Department of Pharmaceutical Sciences (*http://www.ncbi.nlm.nih.gov/pubmed/14745455*) at Northeastern University, Boston determined that a novel growth factor signaling pathway regulates methionine synthase (MS) activity and thereby modulates methylation reactions. The potent inhibition of this pathway by ethanol, lead, mercury, aluminum, and thimerosal suggests that it may be an important target of neurodevelopmental toxins.

• A study published in the *Journal of Child Neurology* (*http://jcn.sagepub.com/content/22/11/1308.abstract*) examined the question of what is leading to the apparent increase in autism. They expressed that if there is any link between autism and mercury, it is crucial that the first reports of the question are not falsely stating that no link occurs. Researchers determined that a significant relation does exist between the blood levels of mercury and the diagnosis of an autism spectrum disorder.

• A study published in the *Journal of Child Neurology* (*http://jcn.sagepub.com/content/21/2/170.abstract*) noted that autistic spectrum disorders can be associated with mitochondrial dysfunction. Researchers determined that children who have mitochondrial-related dysfunctional cellular energy metabolism might be more prone to undergo autistic regression between 18 and 30 months of age if they also have infections or immunizations at the same time.

• A study conducted by Massachusetts General Hospital (*http://www.ncbi.nlm.nih.gov/pubmed/16151044*) at the Centre for Morphometric Analysis by the department of Pediatric Neurology illustrates how autistic brains have a growth spurt shortly after birth and then slow in growth a few short years later. Researchers have determined that neuroinflammation appears to be present in autistic brain tissue from childhood through adulthood. The study excerpt reads:

- Oxidative stress, brain inflammation and microgliosis have been much documented in association with toxic exposures including **various heavy metals.** The awareness that the brain as well as medical conditions of children with autism may be conditioned by chronic biomedical abnormalities such as inflammation opens the possibility that meaningful biomedical interventions may be possible well past the window of maximal neuroplasticity in early childhood because the basis for assuming that all deficits can be attributed to fixed early developmental alterations in net.

- A study conducted by the Department of Pediatrics at the University of Arkansas (*http://www.ncbi.nlm.nih.gov/ pubmed/15527868*) determined that thimerosal-induced cytotoxicity was associated with the depletion of intracellular glutathione (GSH) in both cell lines. The study outlines how many vaccines have been neurotoxic, especially to the developing brain. Depletion of GSH is commonly associated with autism. Although thimerosal has been removed from most children's vaccines, it is still present in flu vaccines given to pregnant women, the elderly and to children in developing countries.

- A study published in the *Public Library of Science (PLOS) (http:// www.plosone.org/article/info%3Adoi%2F10.1371%2Fjournal.*

pone.0068444) determined that elevation in peripheral oxidative stress is consistent with, and may contribute to, more severe functional impairments in the ASD group. We know that oxidative stress is triggered by heavy metals, like the ones contained in multiple vaccines.

• A study conducted by the University of Texas Health Science Centre (*http://www.ncbi.nlm.nih.gov/pubmed/16338635*) by the Department of Family and Community Medicine determined that for each 1,000 lb of environmentally released mercury, there was a 43 percent increase in the rate of special education services and a 61 percent increase in the rate of autism. Researchers emphasized that further research was needed regarding the association between environmentally released mercury and developmental disorders such as autism.

• A study published in the *International Journal of Toxicology* (*http://www.ncbi.nlm.nih.gov/pubmed/12933322*) determined that in light of the biological plausibility of mercury's role in neurodevelopment disorders, the present study provides further insight into one possible mechanism by which early mercury exposures could increase the risk of autism.

• A study published in the *Journal of Toxicology and Environmental Health* (*http://www.ncbi.nlm.nih.gov/pubmed/17454560*) determined that mercury exposure can induce immune, sensory, neurological, motor, and behavioral dysfunctions similar to traits defining or associated with ASDs. Based upon differential diagnoses, 8 of 9 patients examined were exposed to significant mercury from thimerosal-containing vaccine preparations during their fetal/infant developmental periods. These previously normal developing children suffered mercury encephalopathies that manifested with clinical symptoms consistent with regressive ASDs. Evidence for mercury intoxication should be considered in the differential diagnosis as contributing to some regressive ASDs.

• A study published by the US National Library of Medicine (*http://civileats.com/wp-content/uploads/2009/01/palmer2008.pdf*) conducted by the University of Texas Health Science Centre suspected that persistent low-dose exposures to various environmental toxicants including mercury, that occur during critical windows of neural development among genetically susceptible children, may increase the risk for developmental disorders such as autism.

• A study conducted by the Department of Obstetrics and Gynecology (*http://www.ane.pl/pdf/7020.pdf*) at University of Pittsburgh's School of Medicine showed that macaques are commonly used in pre-clinical vaccine safety testing. Collective Evolution does not support animal testing, we feel there is a large amount of evidence and research that already indicated the links to vaccines in which some animals have been used to illustrate. The objective of this study was to compare early infant cognition and behavior with amygdala size and opioid binding in rhesus macaques receiving the recommended childhood vaccines. The animal model, which examines for the first time, behavioral, functional, and neuromorphometric consequences of the childhood vaccine regimen, mimics certain neurological abnormalities of autism. These findings raise important safety issues while providing a potential model for examining aspects of causation and disease pathogenesis in acquired disorders of behavior and development.

• A study conducted by the George Washington University School of Public Health (*http://www.ncbi.nlm.nih.gov/pubmed/18482737*) from the Department of Epidemiology and Biostatistics determined that significantly increased rate ratios were observed for autism and autism spectrum disorders as a result of exposure to mercury from thimerosal-containing vaccines.

• A study published in the journal *Cell Biology and Toxicology* (*http://www.ncbi.nlm.nih.gov/pubmed/19357975*) by Kinki University in Osaka, Japan determined that in combination with the brain pathology observed in patients diagnosed with autism, the present study helps to support the possible biological plausibility for how low-dose exposure to mercury from thimerosal-containing vaccines may be associated with autism.

• A study published by the *Journal Lab Medicine* (*http://labmed.ascpjournals.org/content/33/9/708.full.pdf*) determined that vaccinations may be one of the triggers for autism. Researchers discovered that substantial data demonstrates immune abnormality in many autistic children consistent with impaired resistance to infection, activation of inflammatory responses and autoimmunity. Impaired resistance may predispose to vaccine injury in autism.

• A study published in the journal *Neurochemical Research* (*http://www.ncbi.nlm.nih.gov/pmc/articles/PMC3264864/?tool=pubmed*) determined that since excessive accumulation of extracellular glutamate is linked with excitotoxicity, data implies that neonatal exposure to thimerosal-containing vaccines might induce excitotoxic brain injuries, leading to neurodevelopmental disorders.

Now, imagine, if these studies prove true, all of these varied possibilities of effects on the body and subtle energy system of a small child—your small child. The potential for alteration and damage becomes not only concerning, but terrifying! It also seems quite obvious that our studies must get more focused and that swift action be taken in order to avoid long-term destruction of the bodies, minds, and souls of future generations.

There are two sides to the vaccine issue. This is a volatile subject to say the least. When it comes to your child's health, you must make your own choices based upon your own beliefs. Just be well informed. Ask questions. Require answers. There is a great deal of denial that vaccines cause problems, but there are too many families struggling to put the pieces back together after their child changed dramatically after receiving their immunizations to ignore this subject. We must require that these issues be not only addressed in long-term studies, but that they be remedied immediately.

CHAPTER 9

What Can We Do for Our Children of Now?

As Individuals

When we come from a healthy inner place, our world looks and responds quite differently for us. In relation to the Children of Now, in fact to any child, we do them the very best service when we deal with our issues and get to know ourselves intimately. Once we have that firm base, what we communicate to our children gives them good, healthy examples.

The greatest service we can give the Children of Now is to first get to know ourselves, to drop all of our defenses, and to learn to be authentic. Simply put, we must accept ourselves as who we are and acknowledge our innate perfection. The only way we are ever not perfect is based on our own skewed perceptions. We can be nothing less than perfect because each of us is an aspect of our source—creation reflected as a human being.

We tend to teach children by our actions more so than our words. When we act or react from our self-defenses rather than in an authentic way, we teach our children our dysfunctional patterns. The Children of Now require honesty. They can read us when we aren't truthful. When we don't take the time to answer their questions with honesty, they learn that lying is sometimes okay. Of course, this recognition is on a subconscious, internal level, but it is there nonetheless.

I wrote a sassy book a couple of years ago called *The Art of Living Out Loud* (Weiser Books, 2012). It is the culmination of the questions I have been most frequently asked. No matter where I am in the world, people have the same burning questions about life and our purpose. In the book I provided terrific exercises that we can do to find our way out of the patterns our self-defenses dictate in our everyday lives. Those patterns tend to run our show from the background, on the subconscious level, and most of the time we aren't even aware that we are operating that way. We just fool ourselves into a glossed over set of perceptions that aren't true saying that we are somehow unsafe. Most of what we defend against isn't real. The good news is that we can learn to do things differently.

Once we can be authentic and honest with ourselves, then we can begin to develop some great life skills. When we aren't acting out of self-defense, we are behaving truthfully. When we do that, well, there is nothing left to hide or defend. We don't spend precious life energy on things that aren't even real. We are safe and sincere. When we can be comfortable—really comfortable—with who we are, then we can teach our children to be at ease in the world. And then they will also be at ease in all types of relationships.

We must stop living our lives with fear in the lead. Fear helps us develop untruths. In fact, fear is nothing but a "what-if" anyway! If we can learn to choose from our heart while feeling safe to do so, our choices begin to serve us in ways we can't even imagine from a place of fear.

These days we have become so busy just trying to keep up with life. We have so much coming at us that we get desensitized and lose touch with our feelings and, worse, our passions. Often when I ask someone what their passion is, they look at me blankly and honestly can't say. Passion is nothing more than love in action. It is everything that we love, anything that we do or experience that opens our heart and causes the energy there to expand, filling our chest with the most exquisite feeling. To get back in touch with your passion, start doing little things that give you that feeling. A walk in the woods, a new puppy, a good movie, an intimate conversation with someone you love or with yourself—whatever opens your heart, start doing that so that your feeling self can come back to the surface.

Question everything. You know a whole lot more than you think you do. Get informed about what is important to you and what affects your life. And if whatever that is is challenged, be prepared to stand up and express your opinion.

Express yourself. Do it honestly, calmly, and without feeling threatened. Do it with a sense of humor and drag that sense of humor everywhere that you go. Don't be afraid to use it when appropriate—but not to hurt others. What I mean here is laugh. A lot. Recognize the innocent humor in everything. Don't take things so seriously.

Don't be afraid or resistant to change. How can we evolve at all if we dig our feet into the sand? Change is a great thing. It brings out unseen possibilities.

Be intentional. Do what you mean and mean what you say, and do it all knowing that each and every thing that you do affects all other things. Every action that you take will have an equal reaction, and at some point, that reaction will meet you in your future.

Have it all. Don't feel as if you must limit yourself or dole out the great stuff a little at a time. You deserve whatever you desire. Be willing to accept whatever your desire is when it comes.

We must realize that our purpose isn't a singular moment in our lives, but rather every moment that we live. In each and every moment we exchange energy with everything and everyone around us. We may never know how, in a split second, we touched someone's life, or they, ours.

The next thing that we can do to help our Children of Now is to change how we view them. We tend to observe kids from old ways of thinking. They should be seen and not heard, or currently, we teach them to overachieve so that they have some made-up value that in the long run means nothing but heartache—because to make kids competitive belies not only their sensitivities, but their truth.

Instead, we must realize that they are souls who have come to the planet to have the experience of life. Each child will have their own views of our world and how everyone and everything works together. They will also develop views of how they fit in relation to everything. That is where we come in. If we continue to try and force our own illusions on them, we are doing them a huge disservice.

Now that doesn't mean don't teach them great values. What it means is teach them how to be great human beings. To do that, come from a heartfelt place of sensitivity by really knowing who you are.

As individuals we must heal any remnant family issues that we have. If we don't, we teach our children to repeat in their generations what we couldn't fix in ours.

We must stand up for our Children of Now and demand that they receive in every way in every setting exactly what they need not only to survive but to thrive.

And for goodness' sake, learn how to play again. When you can play freely, you can teach your kids—in fact any kids—how to play freely too.

Having this great set of life tools will be a phenomenal example to the Children of Now in your life and to the future world. In the meantime, these tools will bring amazing things to each of you now.

As Families

So your child may not be like everyone else's. That's okay. Celebrate the difference! If they want to speak to you about their prior lives, listen to their stories. If they do things that seem strange, observe what is going on, but give them room to explore those gifts. If others stare or feel a need to comment on your child, be a loving mirror for them. People who criticize are often afraid of what they don't know.

When it comes to the Children of Now, there are a number of possibilities that a family today may feel thrust into.

Whether a true Child of Now who displays strange insights, memories, and abilities, or one who came brilliantly into our world only to be affected by things unseen to become different in some way, our children are our children.

The greatest message that I want to convey to all families and caregivers is that no matter what type of Child of Now you have, *these children are not broken. They are differently abled.* They are children of God, of creation, of the Universe—whatever your belief system—that are ultimately reflections of light come to earth embodied to blaze with all their might. Some just do it differently.

Second, *you are not alone.* This is one of the sad realizations I had early on. Families with challenging children seem to encapsulate and feel as if they are the only ones on the planet going through what they face with their children every day. That is just not so. In fact, there are countless families who bravely meet the same challenges day in and day out. You need support—and not the kind that carries negative connotations about your child. You should get the kind of support that shines a light on what is good and perfect about your child and his or her journey to our wonderful world.

Don't only listen to medical professionals. Listen deeply to your child, even if that child is one who doesn't speak. You can still hear with your heart. Don't let people tell you that what you see is all there is when it comes to your child. Dig deeper. Find the answers you need, and never, ever give up.

Rearing any type of child is hard work. It is a huge responsibility. You are specialists. True, children don't come with instructions, but the more time you spend learning who you are and getting comfortable with that, the easier it will be to work with your children.

When your child speaks, listen with every part of yourself. Hear what they are saying and don't rush to judgment. These kids are often wise beyond their years. If your child is one who doesn't speak for whatever reason, he or she is still communicating with you. Instead of trying so hard to hear in the ways most of us talk, listen with the ears of your heart. Your child says volumes beyond this plane.

Children are not lesser versions of adults. They are little souls who have come to our planet to have the experience of life. These little souls need guidance. They need to learn the value of themselves beyond a shadow of a doubt. This is one place where getting our own stuff worked out really helps. If we are strong and healthy on the inside, then that is what we will teach our children.

Maintain an environment that is pleasant, comfortable, uncluttered, and easy to keep under control. Make sure there is plenty of light in your home. Kids thrive when there is less chaos in their visual and aural fields.

Have family time with no electronics, no TV, no distractions. Make time to catch up with each other every day. Every single day.

Monitor your child's computer, Internet and social networking content, and the amount of time online. This may be a bone of contention with some of you, but kids are more likely to post their feelings publically to their friends than to come tell you. There are a lot of mean kids out there, and they may be dissing your child in ways that are really harmful. There are also predators who lurk around trying to snag an innocent child. Often they mask their identity as if they are children too. Stay connected.

Give your child a good predictable framework of boundaries and daily routines. This allows your child to feel safe. Children that deal with a constantly changing structure, or none at all, are left to fend for themselves and do not learn all of the life skills they need. When a child knows what to expect, there is a much greater inner calm and sense of surety. Sure, sometimes it is impossible to stick to a routine, but once in a while veering away with an explanation is not a problem.

Just because your child may seem to embody the wisdom of the ages does not mean that she or he should be put on a pedestal or left alone to find a way through the world. Remember the Children of Now are still kids, and they need to learn how to function well and safely. Children who don't learn to respect others will not later respect themselves.

Tell your children the truth in terms they can understand. Don't give stock answers and keep on going. Stop and really see them. They really see you. Don't react, engage. Share your heart with them, your dreams, your own light. What is not spoken leaves doubts in the heart of a child. Think about how much you know about your own parents as human beings. It likely isn't much. If it is, you are one of the lucky few.

Let go of the stereotypes of what being a parent is. Get creative. Honor your children in every way so that they learn to honor others. Remember that children learn more from what is not said than they ever do from what is. It is by example that all roles are taught.

Stick up for your children and don't take whatever they do or say personally. *What your child does is not who you are.* Have a sense of humor. Be willing to listen to all sides, especially your child's before reacting or engaging in solutions. This is especially important at school if your child is accused of some sort of unacceptable behavior. What is behind it? Are others involved? Is there something you didn't know that maybe puts your child at risk of bullying or other issues? Learn everything you can and *then* decide how to deal with the situation.

Your children have interests that excite them. Help them pursue those. Don't push a child to do what you wished you had done! If children are taught to follow their passion, then their passion will become a lifelong pursuit. They won't be looking up when they hit their thirties and wondering what they have accomplished. They will be doing what they love and loving what they are doing.

Your child is a soul who has come to the earth for the experience of life. As soul beings, our children make choices that we may not agree with, especially as they get older. Do your best to teach your children the basics of life and living and give them enough space to exercise their free will to make choices. Let your children understand that every choice has an outcome and an effect. Teach them how to choose well by weighing all of the factors involved.

Communicate, communicate, communicate! Have a heart-to-heart relationship with your children. Learn all about them. Know their dreams, their aspirations, their fears, and support them in everything. Talk with your children of your own inner feelings. This may be hard at first, because we don't always know what we are covering up on a daily basis.

Know yourself, know your child.

Children that can openly communicate without fear of repercussions are children who become good problem solvers and aren't afraid to speak their heart. Children who can talk openly to their parents are better adjusted and calm. This does not mean be your child's best friend and share all of everything. There is a balance. When your child tries to talk with you, don't be quick to criticize or make excuses because whatever is said doesn't seem like a big deal. To kids, everything is a big deal.

You might only get one chance to hear something very important from your children. If you shut them down because you don't have time or an answer, you will miss an opportunity to be of great help to them. Listen carefully, consider what they have said, and then respond with your heart of hearts. Sometimes kids just aren't sure what they need and a little calm logic can go a long way for them.

Trust them. Honor them. If you must criticize, do it with the information about how they could do it differently next time.

Don't be intimidated by your child. You are the parent and your child will love you, honest. If you hesitate to correct your child, find yourself holding your breath, tensing up, whatever, look inward for what part of you is lacking confidence and work on that. Your child needs your guidance. Think of yourself as a temporary Spirit Guide.

Do not allow *anyone for any reason* to tell you what is best for your child. Only you know that. If you don't, ask questions and find out what you need to know.

Teach your child that having isn't value and that being is everything. Stuff isn't important and doesn't fill real needs. Stuff doesn't make children who they are or put them ahead in the competition. Every day in our world the media is thrusting things at us and telling us what kind of person we will be if we use or wear certain products. This puts an enormous amount of pressure on kids to keep up. Kids need to realize that everything they are is on the inside and that life isn't a competition. What kind of person they are in the world will determine how others treat them. No matter how gifted or different your children are, they have value beyond measure. Make sure they know that.

Do everything in your power to limit the kinds of movies and games your children engage with. Reality is crossing boundaries via special effects and great graphics. The scenes and activities are so real these days that they are blurring children's sense of life and death, of war and conflict. There is always another life or a happy ending when the hero gets back up scathed only momentarily as he recharges and goes on to win. That doesn't happen in life. Dead is dead. You can tell your children that but when they are immersed in these kinds of games and watching movies that are beyond their years, they will lose the sense of fear around these subjects. I can't state this strongly enough. Watch what your child's senses consume. Whatever that is, is at risk to come out in behaviors.

Don't let your children isolate. A little time alone is a good thing, but children who are always in their room or somewhere alone are not having healthy relationships in the world. Isolation can lead to internal issues that don't come out. When those issues don't get expressed, they fester or get transferred to a fantasy world, and when that happens, your child may be in jeopardy. The problem is that you won't notice. Be aware of where your children are and what they are doing and with whom. If your children are spending too much time alone, take them somewhere, come up with ideas of places and activities that might interest or enrich them. And don't take no for an answer.

Children have free will just like adults do. Sometimes their will can be intimidating even to the best of parents. Remember that you are a guide and they need your help even when they say they don't. Sometimes they say no when they really mean yes.

Be informed. Know what is happening in the life of your children. If they are of the vaccine age, ask your doctor for the vaccine batch number and go to the vaccine website provided in the resources part of this book. Make sure of what your child is getting and if they in fact need it.

Know your food sources. Everything discussed about GMOs and the resulting physical challenges is true. Why feed your child stuff that causes a constant autoimmune reaction or sets them up for obesity and diabetes? Why feed your child something that may lower brain functioning? Get informed.

Don't forget to ask questions. Take that time. Everything to do with your child is not up to anyone else even though our system is set up to look that way. Yes, it truly takes a village, but our current system allows for a lot of kids to fall through the cracks and not get what they need. Observe your child, ask as many questions as you need, but also listen for the answers.

Mostly, love your child with all your might. You are doing great. The fact that you doubt yourself speaks to the real and sincere desire you have to be a great parent. Stop worrying about it and be that. The best way to get there is to know yourself. That takes a bit of work, but the outcome is always magnificent. Sharing your child's young life can be the greatest experience of *both* of your lives.

As a Society

We like to think of ourselves as civilized people but what kind of civilization turns a blind eye on glaring traits in its kids? As a society we must immediately come to grips with the fact that the Children of Now are highly sensitive beings. When these sensitivities go unnoticed and unacknowledged by the culture at large, the outcome is devastating. Just because something is different doesn't make it a problem. Children are falling through the cracks regularly, and in the process a lot of long-term damage is being done. Some of that damage is irreversible.

In order for society to get our act together, we must come up with a system that makes people accountable for their actions. We have laws that take care of many issues, mostly crimes, but there is a gray area when it comes to our children. Not only are the signals mixed, but there are also social stigmas and public interpretations that damage parents doing their best to make things work for their children.

It has become a problem if your child acts out in public. It is also a problem if you discipline your child in public. In some areas, the act of a parent giving a child a spanking may actually result in that parent being arrested for child abuse. Had that child been allowed to carry on the unacceptable behavior, the parent would have likely been ostracized or asked to leave the premises. Society is sending terribly mixed signals to its members on a regular basis.

Bullying has become another dangerous avenue for kids. It appears that lawmakers and those "in charge" are not acting on suspected bullying instances until a child is hurt or, worse, commits suicide. In previous times bullying never went this far because there was no social networking or Internet to facilitate the mass dissemination of hurtful lies that can completely demolish a child's self-image and reputation.

On top of that, schools are so crowded it is easier for bullying episodes to go unnoticed. When we are dealing with children who are as sensitive as the Children of Now, no level of bullying can be skipped over. Leaving kids to "work it out" just doesn't cut it. Some kids can let meanness by other kids roll off their backs with little or no long-term harm. But the sensitive ones are likely to suffer immensely at the hands of the common bully. What might have been a small interpersonal disagreement or criticism years ago has become an all-out war on a target kid as the traditional single bully is multiplied into a group. We must get to a no tolerance attitude toward bullying. Period.

Anyone who is in charge of children must attend mandatory training on how to spot and deal with the issues kids have. This type of training could be easily developed and implemented. Even those volunteering should have some basic instruction. No matter who they are or what position they hold, anyone who supervises or teaches children must have a clear understanding of the nuances of what a child in jeopardy looks like, such as telltale signs like becoming too quiet or when a great kid suddenly starts acting out or holding his or her head down or avoiding certain children. There are a number of markers that anyone trained in this venue could readily share.

At no time should we allow gangs of kids to congregate or loiter together. When children do this, they develop a hierarchy and a set of behaviors that can become damaging or destructive to others. Usually this kind of dynamic also includes targeting other children who don't have as much confidence or social standing. Once in motion these types of dynamics can escalate out of control with someone getting hurt in some way. At the very least the target may lose lunch money or some other belongings.

Kids that begin to congregate publicly with nothing better to do are insidious. Their numbers tend to grow, and soon there is a community problem. In Spokane, Washington, we have been dealing with just such a problem. Moderate numbers of adolescents have been hanging out at the mall entrance and up and down the streets downtown. They have accosted many people, and there have been several murders as fights got out of hand. For people in general, walking around downtown has become intimidating, and for storefront workers, it is often difficult or threatening to walk to or from their cars at night.

Add to this scenario drug problems, homeless people, and other dynamics and you end up with a ticking time bomb. Spokane is working toward solutions for this very thing, but it has been slow in coming. The situation there is a perfect example of how gathering into gangs of any kind leads to unhealthy dynamics.

We have become extremely competitive people. With limited resources available to us in the way of jobs, money, and other necessities to sustain ourselves, we work harder, longer, and do our best to compete with everyone else who might get in the way of our goals. That lifestyle translates to pressure on kids to accomplish something and to be the best at it too. So many kids are competing for fewer titles or rewards it means all but the champion go home feeling as if they have failed. One might argue that kids need to learn to be competitive if they are to make it in the world, but on the other hand, making it in the world does not require doing so at the expense of others. Instead, learning to work as teams, to rely on each other, and to push for the good of everyone involved teaches respect, good work ethics, and promotes a successful outcome based upon the contributions of each person.

We have set a domain of distraction for our children in activities that have way too much going on with no real depth of experience. Inundated by too many colors, sounds, visuals, possibilities, technologies, pretty soon no kid knows how to feel, and everything becomes a comparison of what was the greatest experience. Soon the experiences do not feel fulfilling because they are all attacking the senses and not feeding the heart or the mind. There are places that specialize in this exact type of thing such as (and not to pick on anyone in particular) storefronts that are nothing but a huge room of video games, music, toys, and animated robotic characters doing shows with the noise of all of the games running over it all. Announcements are being made, and on top of that they are serving food and drinks and calling people up for their orders. Having birthday parties in these types of places has become a status symbol. There are balloons everywhere to mark party areas, and no one could carry on a conversation if they wanted to. Just trying to maintain attention on where your child ran off to is nearly impossible.

Pretty much all places and spaces that offer activities for kids are some version of this. The idea seems to be more, larger, louder, better, higher, busier, etc. It all costs money that is quickly spent, and there is no real humanity to this kind of experience. It feels more like desperation to have a good time with nothing really to show at the end of the day except a lot of money spent and maybe a few cheap souvenirs quickly lost or broken.

These kinds of environments rob the humanity of our kids and push them into fantasy. It makes the kids frenetic. Sure, these kinds of places are great if the parents just want to go let the kids run in a contained area, but honestly, is there a connection between people in them? They are all designed for the surface experience, instant gratification, and no long-term benefit.

Of course, there are some really great places to take kids designed for hands-on learning. For instance, the aquarium in Atlanta is magnificently planned for families to experience together. The layout is conducive to a good foot traffic flow, there are employees everywhere to answer questions, the environment is pleasant, even exciting, and it has heart. Some zoos have great hands-on areas as well. These are types of environments in which children can learn the value of our ecosystems, nature, and the immensity of balance our natural world requires. Such impressions will go a long way toward their attitudes in the future.

In Schools

Kids spend more of their waking time in school than anywhere else. Because of this, school plays a huge role in the shaping of our children's lives. Children learn values from other kids at school and through what is taught there. Unfortunately as communities we have not allowed for enough funding or attention on our school systems, so proper training and even everyday supplies are lacking.

We need to revamp our perceptions of school. From the parent's end, we trust that when we send our child to school he or she will be in good hands and have everything needed for learning, but the truth is, that really isn't the case on the whole. We can't take it for granted that the school systems are appropriately managed and that employees have everything required to do a great job with our kids. We must completely reassess how our schools are managed, what funding they need, and how to get it, and then implement some social conditions that foster the mental health of our children.

Generally speaking, our school curricula are based on a system that is more than a hundred years old. It was designed in times when family values were taken for granted and schools were very small, incorporating all grades and experience levels. Our school systems have evolved into monstrosities of compartmentalized management and thinking, and in the United States we are watching them go down the tubes.

For instance, according to an article by Ben Shapiro on Breitbart News, *80 percent of New York city children can't read when they graduate from high school.* Here are some more statistics that will scare the heck out of you as posted on Statisticbrain.com and provided by Read Faster Reading Stats from a study in April 2013:

- Kids with actual reading disorders: 15%

- American adults who can't comprehend the labels on their prescriptions: 46%

- Young people who claim to have read more than ten books a year: 56%

- U.S. adults who are unable to read at even an eighth grade level: 50%

- Amount of words read yearly by someone who reads fifteen minutes each day: 1 million

- Students who will never read another book after high school: 33%

- College students who will never read a book after college: 42%

- U.S. families who didn't buy any books in the last year: 80%

- Adults who haven't been in a bookstore in the last five years: 70%

- Books started but not finished: 57%

What is happening? In our country there is very little emphasis on school and any studies beyond high school. Many families are just trying to survive since our economy has become a have and have-not society. We have evolved a dumbed down emphasis on schools with even less funding. Many schools do not have enough books or other supplies to go around. In California, 85 percent of schools lack an accredited librarian.

Currently, 8.1 percent of kids—meaning more than 8,300 per day—drop out of school. This adds up to a total of *over three million dropouts every year.* Why don't they stay? What is keeping them there? What do we do for kids to make them want to stay in school? Granted there are some occasions when children leave school for health, family, or financial reasons, but they are nowhere near the majority.

We must revisit what we offer children from kindergarten on up.

In addition, we must immediately put in place good training for teachers and all involved with the kids to spot and assist children who are having problems or who live life from a fuller set of senses than previous generations.

This will incorporate the Children of Now with their oversensitivities, those with learning disabilities, victims of bullying or other degrading behaviors, and even those who come from problem homes. Not only should we understand and counsel these kids, we must be prepared to offer good acceptable solutions.

To do these things our budgets need to be revamped, and our different federal, state, and local governments must be willing to provide funding to make things work. It is a travesty that our schools do not have what they need. We are turning into a country of unskilled, uneducated people. If we do not have the education to make informed decisions, we will continue to allow ourselves to be led by others. If we haven't a clue what is going on, we can be corralled up any path anyone with a little education decides to take us.

It is certainly possible for our budgets to be revamped. What it will take is reconsidering our priorities. Huge amounts of money are wasted every minute on poor management structure and overextended bureaucratic ideas of how many people it takes to do any task. If we were to streamline the management of our educational systems starting at the very top and then evolve our education requirements to a set of skills with real-world applications, then maybe we could begin to give our kids what they really need.

In addition to revamping the management hierarchy of our school systems, we must adapt our curricula to include life skills courses beginning from kindergarten on up. These might cover interpersonal relationships—dealing with problems of an internal nature—how to deal with real-life situations, money management, family values, and any other subjects that will give our children a good start on life. School has devolved to fiscal concerns, and those on the ground don't have what they need to do a great job. They are overrun, stressed by the behaviors of some of their students, and powerless to discipline them when they act out.

All of that being said, how do we specifically help the Children of Now, those who are highly sensitive, feeling everything around them as if it were their own, and experiencing discomfort because their environments aren't conducive to anything else?

We can begin by accepting that not all perceived learning disabilities are actually that. Some kids learn differently than others, but that doesn't mean they are disabled. It just means that they need us to bend toward what they do need. Kids are being pigeonholed into specific categories that have a negative connotation with regard to their intelligence. They are being labeled with any number of disorders such as ADD and ADHD. Too many kids are thrust into special ed classes because their performance isn't up to par. The real questions are why are they behind and what will it take to get them to where they need to be? Throwing them into a less challenging environment is only going to serve to degrade them until they have lost self-respect and any sense of value.

What if these kids are being slowly and intrinsically destroyed by our methods? What if there is nothing wrong with them? What if what is really happening is that we, through ignorance, are forcing our expectations upon them and, because of evolutional differences, they are not able to comply in any manner we assume is correct?

What if our children simply require us to learn and use different methods? Different environments? What if in all of our well-meaning efforts we are tearing down the confidence and long-term productivity of the very children we mean to help?

In this time not all children are created equally, so how can we expect them to act as if they are?

Many of the Children of Now are highly intelligent and easily bored in traditional class settings. Their lightning minds process information immediately while others in their class struggle to keep up. Some are so affected by their school environment and those around them that they do poorly in class. The situation is a conundrum to be sure. One solution is to evaluate kids not only on what they already know but on social skills and sensitivities. It can be done. There are ways to assess kids to see where they stand on sensitivities without analyzing them or making them feel as if they are being graded like eggs. A good conversational-type evaluation would assist in determining the needs children *before* placing them into a challenged position.

Besides training staff to recognize and assist the various types of kids, it would be a super idea if every class had a powwow discussion in which kids can safely share their perceptions and problems in the classroom. Kids aren't allowed to talk enough or express their opinions. Instead they are required to regurgitate lessons learned by rote. But who are these little people? How do they feel about life and all of its happenings? What is in their hearts? Does anyone care about the internal development of these kids or is everything funneled to fit an educational model that is archaic and perhaps destructive? There is an "I AM" in every child, and we owe it to them to learn just who that is!

Sometimes just getting kids to talk about things eases their anxiety tremendously. We say that kids say the darndest things, but honestly, what they say isn't novel, it is their perception of the world around them that we have created for them.

The key to this would be that the staff would need to be great listeners to hear the meaning between their words and to act on that if necessary. If kids could learn good problem solving in class, it would go a long way toward reducing disciplinary issues at school.

As part of her doctoral dissertation, my friend Angela gave a digital recorder to her students and asked them what wisdom they would like to share with the world. The results were stunning. What the kids had to say was simple, profound, heartfelt, and wise. When she defended her dissertation, the kids comments were the very last part of her presentation. The panel and the audience were in tears as they listened to the unabashed sentiments of her students. This type of exercise should be incorporated throughout the schools so that we can begin to realize just who it is we are teaching and move from teaching just the facts to bringing a well-rounded full mentorship program to our students.

Many might argue that there are just too many kids and not enough time or staff. I say, then fix it. It isn't the kids' fault that our education system is in the condition that it is. With the statistics the way they are, the state of our education system speaks to the very lack of education of our general population. This leaves a blessed few trying to do it all, and they are overwhelmed.

There are great teachers out there: those who see the need to expand the human side of our kids and those who work on the fringes to introduce and implement extras to their programs to expand the growth of our children from all angles. Great kudos to these brave souls!

One of the most important parts of human growth is our creative side. Due to funding concerns many school systems have eliminated art and music classes as less important to the entire scheme of education. How ignorant is *that!* The curricula are so fragmented and compartmentalized that education is sadly evolving into a hit-and-miss kind of thing.

Our brains have both a logical and a creative side. For a child to develop fully, both sides of the brain must be not only stimulated, but also exercised. Music and art are the language of the soul!

Physical education has suffered for many of our kids as it has been taken out of or limited in scope within our schools. At a time when children are weighing more than ever and at risk for diabetes and other health issues, they are not being given the exercise and physical challenges that they need to become healthy people. So what if we fill their brains? If they don't have the motivation or physical strength to carry out what they have learned, what have we achieved?

Another issue that we have is the abundance of performance testing. It has become continual. We test them for things like BMI (body mass index), fitness levels, IQ, skills in math, English, and other subjects. In every case of testing, some students are stigmatized as either champions or less than failures, or in need of something more. Unfortunately, these tests serve to stigmatize children and frankly stress them out.

These tests take a huge amount of time to be scored, evaluated as a whole, and assessed for any future action to be implemented to correct weaknesses in the system. By the time the data is assimilated and interpreted and recommendations are made, the kids who took those tests are often years along in school.

If children were allowed to feel full and whole instead of treated and graded (or degraded), perhaps their learning processes would show that by way of successful results. If they had a different perspective of doing their best instead of being the best, perhaps they really would.

Our focus has been on winning and succeeding, and this leads to hypercompetitiveness or failure. Can we not accept the child who is quieter, more sensitive, just as easily as we accept the one who shines the brightest by knowing how to play the game? Do we not see that we are recreating the very world in which we find ourselves uncomfortable? If we are to change our world for the future of our children, we must first gain the awareness that we have the power to instigate and propagate those changes.

How children learn has transformed. With all of the information coming at them every day, their minds have evolved to quickly assess and file data. The Children of Now absorb information like sponges. It goes into their wonderfully compartmentalized minds and comes out if and when it is needed. In the meantime they might appear as if they are in pure chaos and learning nothing. This assumption is so wrong.

If some children are not thriving in a structured environment such as our classrooms, then perhaps it is time to back off of the structure and its expectations and allow them to find the way with some good direction. There is a lot to be learned, for instance, as children go into a breakout for a project or activity. As they gather in their groups, certain dynamics occur that allow validation of each other, consideration of the ideas of others, real-world experience in how to get along with each other, an awareness that everyone's contribution matters. In fact there are so many benefits from those small moments.

If we were able to create a classroom environment that strengthened children as people, giving them not only the knowledge they need but also the skills to advance in our world, we would be contributing to the future in ways that will benefit coming generations beyond measure.

There are less structured teaching methods such as the wheel system I suggested in *The Children of Now*. For instance, if children were to receive a list of assignments due at structured times such as within one hour, one day, one week, whatever, and then had a central place to access everything they needed to complete that assignment, this would alleviate the necessity for so many books and extraneous supplies. Kids could move freely through this system achieving their goals and feeling really good about themselves.

They would also feel much calmer not being confined to chairs and desks all day. The environment could be much less formal, allowing for children to sit on the floor if desired or to put their feet up. Physical comfort contributes a considerable amount toward the willingness of a student to delve deeper into any subject.

The freedom to move about would mitigate a large percentage of the ADD/ADHD behaviors since the kids would be able to shake off some of the energy built up in their bodies. Energy buildup can feel very physical and uncomfortable—as if you have been plugged into an electrical socket with no off button. Movement helps. Open communication and a regard for everyone equally as part of that communication are vital for the growth of our children.

The old paradigm is that children should sit at attention with their feet on the floor in silence unless spoken to. In the current world, this idea is ludicrous! It is a paradox: there are huge volumes of information coming at kids all of the time, and then we expect them to be still like inert containers and do nothing with that but what we tell them. Seriously?

We must craft a new paradigm of fluidity that fits the world we live in. To do that, we must change how we expect our children to experience school.

As those responsible for the future of our children, we must listen to them. What they have to share is a huge statement on how we are doing. If we are determined to be right, we will miss the pointers kids offer toward what *would* work for them. We must stop acting out our perception of school and start uncovering what that perception really means.

Out of all of this—which if you think about it, is quite simple—one of the most important aspects of raising children is communication. Children who freely speak their hearts are usually healthy children. Those who are not allowed to speak or not heard when they do begin to become internally corrupt. Their senses of self get skewed, and then at some point they become adults with issues. Allowing for children to create positive self-images would go a long way toward alleviating bullying and other inter-personal issues. If children have confidence and a good internal understanding of who they are, they are less susceptible to turning aggressive or being victimized.

Listening deeply is paramount to knowing how we are doing with our children and what they are not getting from us. Communicating with our kids honestly and fully will assist them through the greatest of challenges. The more we interact on a personal level with our children, the less possibility there is of them creating an internal dialogue in a fantasy world about who they wish they were. Allowing children to shine their inner being is a beautiful thing and paramount to our success as educators and therefore mentors for their future lives.

CHAPTER 10

Future World

Something happens around the time Crystalline Children turn ten or eleven years old. It is as if a switch flips and they become socially aware on levels most adults don't even consider. Not only do these kids wake up, they *act*. In addition, our Star Kids are on top of technologies. They have ideas for the future . . . and the present!

Consider these amazing examples:

- When Peter was ten, he noticed that not all of the kids in his school had the same lunches as everyone else in his class. He also noticed that some kids didn't have any lunch. Peter started a food drive to collect donations so that everyone in his school would have the same lunches.

- Eleven-year-old Andrew Pelham learned that around thirty-eight children die every year from being left in hot cars. Andrew decided to do something about it. He invented the E-Z baby saver. It is made out of rubber bands and duct tape and stretches from the backseat across the driver's door. It stops parents in their tracks and reminds them that the baby is with them.

- Eleven-year-old Peyton Robertson, from Fort Lauderdale, Florida, designed a new kind of sandbag to protect against flooding from hurricanes and other disasters. He was really concerned after Superstorm Sandy did so much damage. He wanted to come up with a way that people could be better prepared. His Sandless Operational Sandbag (SOS) earned him the title of "America's 2013 Top Young Scientist" after he won the Discovery Education 3M Young Scientist Challenge.

- In France, young people were upset at the large number of homeless people in their villages. It all started when a ten-year-old boy publicly brought attention to the issue. To him, it was a travesty. Much to the embarrassment of the French government, the youngsters started a group called the Children of Don Quixote (Les Enfants de Don Quichotte). They pitched red tents along the rivers to provide shelter for the homeless. Before long, there were red tents along nearly every river in France.

- In Chhattisgarh, central India, a young boy invented a remarkable device that alerts the inhabitants if someone is trying to barge into their house. The device has a trigger that activates a cellular phone and sends calls and messages to the owner of the house through it.

These are just a few examples of the social conscience and actions of the Children of Now. Not only are their hearts made of gold, they are willing to put themselves out there to make a difference. We have the Crystalline Children, who are all about love and social awareness, and we have the Star Kids, who are all about the earth and technologies that are safer and have exquisite purpose. Together they are the perfect marriage of types of perceptions coming together for the future of our world.

These are children who care about complete strangers. They are kids who support heartfelt causes that affect countless people. These young ones create new inventions so that others benefit. Our next generation is going to take the world by storm.

Imagine a future when conscious, caring human beings get themselves elected to office because they are charismatic, intelligent, farseeing, and willing to stand by their convictions. Think about scientists who move beyond creative and into genius as they come up with technologies that do no harm to the planet and in fact assist in cleaning up the messes that previous generations have left behind.

Crystalline Children and Star Kids are mercifully paired as the future of the world. They will do it well, and they will do things right. They will see to it that everyone on our planet has what they need. They will not let some waste food while others die from a lack of it. They will not allow further damage to our earth from the destruction of fossil fuel production or pollution of the air and water due to factory emissions. They will not allow for certain percentages of pollution to be okay. They will find ways to do better.

As for farming and the exchange of those commodities, the Children of Now will by then have discovered the damage that genetic modification has done to the human body and to the rest of the food chain. They will find that the genetic modification causes mutations in cellular behaviors and functioning, and that this has been much of the reason the autoimmune systems of most people have gone awry. Genetic modification for the purpose of changes in crops will be outlawed.

They will find that herbicides and bug sprays used on crops have caused long-term damage to the human cellular system and caused imbalances in the body that will take countless generations to change. They will also discover that mutations will begin to show up particularly in the skin and in the color of people's eyes. Other mutations will move to the forefront such as interference in our absorption of nutrients. Evidence will also be discovered that genetic modifications have been triggering our autoimmune systems, brain functioning, and endocrine balance, leaving instability of emotions, hormones, and other systems.

They will find that certain chemicals and toxins in the environment have created cellular mutations causing an outbreak of cancer among world populations and at the same time affected bacteria and viruses so that they were immune to normal antibiotic or other treatments.

As new strains of disease appear in the future, our Children of Now will look to the cause and alleviate the effects, but that will take time as by then the damage and long-term evolution of the problems will already be massive. *Organic* will take on an entirely new meaning when the Children of Now become involved with food production. No longer will they allow its definition to vary from country to country or certain impurities in imported foods to be overlooked.

At the same time they will streamline communications even further while finding new and different ways to share technologies. Information will no longer be linear in format. Instead, it will be available as packets that can be plugged together to create specific outcomes or full libraries of information on any number of subjects. Groups of information will be modifiable and selectable so that tailored learning can be achieved.

The Children of Now will have discovered how the brain truly functions and will develop technologies to place information in the brain much like we program computers. The difference will be that the information will also contain the benefit of all applications and their outcomes. In other words, whatever mistakes were made before then will be noted and solutions already in place. The information will come as proven data.

They will create more efficiently but will do so with an attention to the overall effects on our world their production will have.

The Crystallines will lead while the Star Kids create supportive clean technologies that make learning and travel much easier. They will alleviate all nonefficient ways of production and anything that harms our natural world.

No more will we have just a United Nations; we will have a World Coalition. Together the Children of Now will create a collective to distribute commodities across the world in such a way that all countries will be able to share their resources and benefit in exchange by receiving what other countries have produced.

Housing will be constructed from new and specific materials that are earth-friendly but not at the expense of comfort. Materials will be more modular in form and will not contain toxic chemicals in the name of preservation. The Children of Now will come up with new technologies that will allow for altogether new materials for building that will be sustainable, maintainable, and not deteriorate in the way that current materials do.

The Children of Now will ultimately come up with methods to produce infinite energy that is safe, clean, and to the benefit of all people. These new energies will far exceed anything we have known in the past. They will find that as energy is expended, it also creates energy. Up to now we have been a consumptive world. But what if, *what if,* the Children of Now apply their gifts to utilize the very energy that contributes to their inherent sensitivities? Not only will they be able to fuel the world at little to no cost (and therefore even the scales of the economy too), they will be able to apply the same principles to other things as well.

Take medicine, for example. Learning to understand the subtle energy of electromagnetics brings with it an entirely different approach to healing the human body and to preventing illness and disease. Once the subtle energy system is recognized and understood, medical testing as we know it will take on an entire new face. We will be able to scan the body for harmonic insufficiencies or dis-harmonic protocols. They will learn that each and every human's energy field has individual variances but that the norm is within specific ranges. Harmonic adjustments to the system will be used to deal with problems in positive ways without pharmaceutical supplementation. Healing will take on an entirely new identity, as will wellness.

Of course, these changes will come with a price. There will be a period of adjustment between the old and the new. There always is. But the Children of Now are determined, strong souls who will stand up for what they believe in and will act upon whatever the issues are until positive change occurs.

Politics will also take on a new identity and role in our world once our Children of Now are in charge. They will run things efficiently and honestly. Instead of fostering self-serving roles, the children will bring back the true meaning of "We the people" and the true meaning of Oneness. They will not allow for classes to rule as they have in the past, but rather they will strive toward the equality of all nations, all people, and each to the benefit of the whole.

They will also very likely refine world currencies to a singular value system so that all trading can be on equal terms.

They will tend to bring much needed change to over-population.

The Children of Now will tear down racial barriers in the interest of all being supported equally. They will foster honor in diversity toward the benefit of the entirety.

The Children of Now will create new and different educational programs that fit their evolving needs as they continue to advance in their differences. They will also make certain that education is available to all—not only the privileged few.

Schools will take on a modular form, with not only classes on the usual subjects. They will also insist upon students having classes on family values, interpersonal relationships, how to manage money, how to participate in everything they do toward the benefit of all. These types of classes won't be elective; they will be required avenues of study.

Lessons will eventually be able to be tailored for each specific student, and learning will include experiential exercises and infusions of data via downloads to the brain as virtual experiences.

Lack of mutuality will not be tolerated nor will anyone who does anything at the expense of another. The entire societal norm will shift toward respect and commonality.

They won't make the changes by force either. Instead, they will do so with sound logic, honesty, and a solid plan. And people will listen because their limitless caring will show through. Their words will not be rhetoric, but instead, boundless truth that is hard to argue with.

As for the planet, care will be given by the Children of Now that the forces of nature not be altered or ignored. They will have such a deep intrinsic connection with the energy of everything that they will insist upon all things natural being left just that. They will realize that certain technologies interfere with the natural migration of species, and that the migration of those species is responsible for the overall balance of nature. They will see that in all the world, everything has its rhythm and that rhythm is the basis of all life. Life is a precious thing, as is the energy that sustains it.

The Children of Now will be fearless in their pursuits, and whatever they do, they will do as living reflections of a greater One.

What a wonderful world it will be.

In Retrospect

When I wrote *The Children of Now*, I wasn't the only one along for the ride. There were a number of people mentioned in the book including actual children of the various types, their parents and caregivers. It seems only fitting to catch up the current reader with where these children are today.

There were originally four kids in particular who began to talk to me telepathically and all at once. I am being kind. The truth is they hounded me day and night. They had a lot to say. Not only did they shake my world by filling my brain with their voices, thoughts, and pictures that were not my own, they took the world by the tail and commanded to be heard. And heard they were!

I feel it only fitting to give a quick update on the original four. There were and are so many more, but these four souls are indelibly bonded with mine.

Weston

Weston (aka William in *The Children of Now*. In later books we used his real name) was and remains the most powerful telepath I know. He was the first to come into my awareness. Weston interrupted my train of thought so many times it seemed that I wasn't in control of my brain at all. He snuck in on me when I least expected him and not only did he give me thoughts, but visuals as well.

Once I began to hear Weston and made it public, all of a sudden it seemed like everyone could hear Weston. It is funny how when we become aware of a new possibility, all of a sudden it becomes part of the common reality.

Weston was very good not only at telepathically communicating but also at out of body travel. When he and I got together in the ethers for healing sessions or simply to talk with each other, all of a sudden I found myself out of body and traveling to the most amazing places. Weston took me to Atlantis and to the birth of his soul mate far in the distant past. She wasn't currently in our world, but by visiting the past he was able to reconnect with her. His little friend was even more powerful than he was and the two of them together were hard to keep up with!

Weston has a hilarious sense of humor. He very often blanked my mind out then filled it with the craziest stuff like galactic travelers (he had a whole troupe of them). One of them was always with Weston. He was extremely tall— seven or eight feet—and Weston called him, if I remember right, "Oo Loo."

Weston and Oo Loo visited me often. When they came, it was a lot like that bar scene in *Star Wars* with all of the different alien races. Bizarre to say the least, but I have to admit, a real hoot!

At one point Weston had decided it would be great fun to just take me over anytime he wanted. To him, it was hilarious to dive-bomb me with a totally new reality right when I was in mid-thought. One day I was in the recording studio when he filled my head with croaking bullfrogs. It was pretty funny but directly interfered with my recording. I chastised Weston for jumping into my brain knowing that I was in the middle of something very important. After I fussed at him, Weston didn't talk to me for over two months. Talk about etheric pouting!

As more people began to hear Weston, he became very excited and began to talk through others. This all sounds really bizarre, but I assure you it is as true as the day is long. The really stunning thing in all of this was that Marilu, Weston's mom, was not able to hear Weston in the way that some of us could. Talk about uncharted waters for a parent! If ever I have met a great sport, it is Marilu.

Weston came to be so well known through the books that people were contacting Marilu in droves seeking advice, information, delivering messages they believed were from Weston (some actually were). They told her what Weston wanted and what would be good for Weston and . . . whew! Marilu called me one evening when I was on the road and she really needed advice. She was completely overwhelmed and overrun with well-meaning people.

The first thing I told Marilu was that Weston is and will always be her son. Anyone who tried to tell her what was best for Weston had an agenda and it wasn't about Weston or Marilu. With practice, Marilu began to figure out how to filter all of the information and advice that was coming her way. It was a real task since Weston was really stirring the pot. He loved it that people could hear him.

Weston started giving teleconferences by allowing himself to be voiced through a family friend. Not only did they do teleconferences, they also worked together to do actual seminars and weekend workshops!

All along Marilu waited for the otherwise silent Weston to talk with her, but to date he has not. Marilu wrote a marvelous book about the experiences she has had with Weston and how he has always guided her and the rest of the family right to where they needed to be. Their story is absolute magic. The book, called *Waiting for Weston*, is available on Amazon.

Lorrin

Lorrin Danielle Kain, to whom I dedicated this book, was the second child to contact me telepathically. She was a gorgeous little redhead with the hugest blue eyes on the planet. Lorrin wasn't able to speak or use her body the way most kids do. Her physical problems began with a really bad reaction to childhood vaccines. One minute she was a normal little one and not much after that she had crashed.

There had come a time when I was hearing so much in my head—different little voices sometimes all talking at once—that I made a sincerely exasperated request to meet them in person so that I could validate the reality of what I was experiencing. When you do that, you really must be careful what you wish for!

I met Lorrin and her mom Karen in the lobby of the Celebrate Your Life Conference in Scottsdale. I was talking with a friend with my back to the aisle when I heard a little girl say "Hi, I made it!" This was another one of these moments in life where your entire body tells you that things will never be the same.

I knew immediately that Lorrin was one of my four voices. When I told Karen what had been happening, she laughed and said that, yeah, Lorrin talks to everyone. I have to say I was a bit shocked at first and then awed at the ease with which Karen recounted several stories about Lorrin and her telepathic antics. Karen could hear Lorrin. This was a huge relief to me! Karen told me that crazy things would happen around Lorrin. Apparently several people quit smoking after just being in her presence. Others were often healed, or their lives put onto a new and often dramatically positive direction after encountering Lorrin.

Even though Lorrin was basically nonfunctional physically, Karen treated her like any normal child. Lorrin went shopping, had parties, had pizza nights with friends. It was a real lesson in life just being around them.

The first night after I met Lorrin and on many thereafter I was often awakened by her. I would see her dancing like the most gifted ballerina I had ever known. She showed me a room of mirrors reflecting her as she glided across the floor. She told me that when she was out of body, she was free and nothing could stop her from dancing. She told me that maybe one day her physical body could catch up, but it didn't matter if it didn't.

Karen, Lorrin, and I became great friends. I used to visit them at their home near Los Angeles. Every night, Lorrin would either keep me awake or wake me up with visions of her dancing ballet or giggling like every little girl over something silly. To look at her, one would never think all that bubbly fun was cooped up inside of her, but she was a powerhouse.

I introduced Lorrin and her mom to Nicholas and his mom Susan (Nicholas wrote the foreword to *The Children of Now*). Karen sent a photo of Lorrin to the little guy. He was so enamored with Lorrin, they stayed up all night talking telepathically to each other, and Susan finally had to remove Lorrin's photo from his room so that Nicholas would go to sleep. Too funny.

Lorrin lost the ability to breathe on her own, and her health problems deteriorated. No coincidence, I was with them the last week before Lorrin's passing. My room was across the hall from Lorrin's, and I could easily see into where she lay. As she came close to the end, I saw a little spirit boy who looked to be around eight or ten years old. He was dressed in clothing from the 1800s. He had on little knickers, a three-quarter sleeved jacket, and a white shirt. He looked like he was dressed up for a special occasion. It was.

He would come and stand on her bed at night and watch Lorrin very tenderly. It looked like they had known each other forever, or maybe they had been related at some other time. Their rapport was quiet, connected, and somehow peaceful. He held Lorrin with his eyes in the most loving way. The feeling was almost tangible.

One night, Lorrin woke me at 4 a.m. to tell me she was leaving. Her message was profoundly clear and sadly disturbing, as I knew that her passing would be a hard thing for many people, especially her mom. I jumped up and ran into her room expecting her to be gone. She was scarcely there, but yes, still barely breathing with the help of a machine. I have to admit to a moment of sheer confusion at Lorrin still being alive. Her message had shaken my very core. When these kids talk to you in such a pure form, the reality of their communications can affect your entire body, mind, and spirit. Everything in the messages is experienced mentally, physically, emotionally, and spiritually.

The next morning when Lorrin's nurse arrived, she didn't come in quietly as she usually did. Instead she ran through the front door, down the hall, and into Lorrin's room. She was as shocked as I was to see Lorrin still breathing and among the living. Lorrin had also gone to her at exactly 4 a.m. to tell her she was leaving. I finally realized that Lorrin was alerting us so that we could be supportive of her mom when she actually did pass. Lorrin was like that.

A few days later, not long after I left to return home, Lorrin Danielle Kain left the planet and went back to the light laying in her mother's arms. Her last goodbye to me was fleeting. Once free of her body, there was nothing stopping her. She is still missed in so many ways, but somehow when you have been touched by her, Lorrin never really leaves you.

Karen has written a wonderful account of her life with Lorrin in *A Unique Life Fully Lived – The Lorrin Kain Story*. It will be released prior to this book, but as of this writing I do not have the exact date. Look for it on *www.karenkain.com*.

Tristan

Tristan, aka Trevor in *The Children of Now*, is a Star Kid of great gifts and abilities. When I first knew Tristan, he was not talking at all. He had a serious connection with animals, especially his dogs. He was very concerned about the state of the earth. He used to have dreams about being in a white room and then falling. Tristan was a natural-born healer, his insights pure and powerful.

Since I met Tristan and the other kids, I have come across people who somehow know Tristan and his family in many places. It is as if on some level Tristan wanted me to meet his support system. I met his speech therapist and others who have helped him in some way.

As Tristan grew older, he began to speak for the first time in his life—tentatively at first, then in full sentences, and finally conversations. Tristan has opened up in glorious ways. He is determined to help the world and has done many teleconferences and other events. I had the privilege to participate in his teleconferences, and he did a great job.

Tristan has always had immense support from his parents, and they participate with him on his mission. The first time Tristan and I talked in a regular earthbound conversation I wanted to jump for joy knowing that others would hear the sweet heart of this shining young man.

Nicholas

Sweet, sweet Nicholas was nine when he wrote the foreword to *The Children of Now*. When I asked him what the Children of Now needed most, he said that deep listening was the key. A brilliant child of the light, Nicholas was challenged with severe physical issues including cerebral palsy. Nicholas had his own website and had been named a "Love Ambassador" by the Love Foundation (www.thelovefoundation.com), a group dedicated to inspiring unconditional love, because his messages were filled with nothing but kindness and loving sentiments. He was the little guy who had the immense crush on Lorrin.

I am not privy to all of the details, but it is my understanding that the local government took Nicholas from his family, shut down his website, and institutionalized him, re-diagnosing him as mentally retarded. Apparently he is now heavily medicated and not reachable telepathically. How sad this is! If only they knew what an exceptional light he is inside. This news broke my heart for Nicholas.

Unfortunately many of our differently gifted children do not get a fair shake in our world. If they look different, act different, are different, they are considered dysfunctional. I suggest that we look deeper, listen harder, reach inside, and get over the stigma that what is different can't be right. Knowing these beautiful children has taught me to never, ever look away from anyone who is different, but instead to pay closer attention to the gifts they have brought to our world. They are love embodied.

Resources

I have not read or perused every resource listed here; many have been recommended to me through my various sources of research. I include these as a service to the reader. I neither recommend nor necessarily share the views stated in the following books and websites. I basically wanted to offer as many points of view here as possible so that you, the reader, can decide for yourself what is true for you and for your child. I am sure there are many more resources, and I may have forgotten some. I am always interested in what is new and pertinent to the Children of Now. I hope that this list is helpful for you!

Other Books by Meg Blackburn Losey, PhD

The Art of Living Out Loud: How to Leave Behind Your Baggage and Pain to Become a Happy, Whole, Perfect Human Being with Unlimited Potential. Weiser Books, 2012.

The Children of Now: Crystalline Children, Indigo Children, Star Kids, Angels on Earth, and the Phenomenon of Transitional Children. New Page Books, 2006.

Conversations with the Children of Now: Crystal, Indigo, and Star Kids Speak about the World, Life, and the Coming 2012 Shift. New Page Books, 2008.

The Living Light Cards. Weiser Books, 2011.

Parenting the Children of Now: Practicing Health, Spirit, and Awareness to Transcend Generations. Weiser Books, 2009.

Pyramids of Light: Awakening the Multidimensional Realities Spirit Light Resources. 1st edition, 2004.

The Secret History of Consciousness. Weiser Books, 2010.

Touching the Light: 365 Illuminations to Live By. Weiser Books, 2012.

Touching the Light: Healing Mind, Body, and Spirit by Merging with God Consciousness. Weiser Books, 2011.

Books: The Children of Now

Atwater, PMH. *Beyond the Indigo Children.* Bear & Company, 2005.

Atwater, PMH. *Children of the Fifth World.* Bear & Company, 2012.

Atwater, PMH. *Future Memory.* Hampton Roads Publishing; reprint edition, 2013.

Blackburn Losey, Meg. *The Children of Now.* New Page Books, 2006.

Blackburn Losey, Meg. *Conversations with the Children of Now.* New Page Books, 2008.

Blackburn Losey, Meg. *Parenting the Children of Now.* Weiser Books, 2009.

Carrol, Lee, and Tober, Jan. *The Indigo Children: The New Kids Have Arrived.* Hay House; 1st edition, 1999.

Carrol, Lee, and Tober, Jan. *The Indigo Children Ten Years Later: What's Happening with the Indigo Teenagers!* Hay House, 2009.

Miller, Suzy. *AWESOMISM!: A New Way to Understand the Diagnosis of Autism*. iUniverse, 2008.

Autism Books

Aune, Beth, Burt, Beth, and Gennaro, Peter. *Behavior Solutions for the Inclusive Classroom: A Handy Reference Guide that Explains Behaviors Associated with Autism, Asperger's, ADHD, Sensory Processing Disorder, and other Special Needs.* Future Horizons April 30, 2010.

Baker, Jed. *Preparing for Life: The Complete Guide for Transitioning to Adulthood for Those with Autism and Asperger's Syndrome.* Future Horizons; 1st edition, 2006.

Bishop, Beverly. *My Friend with Autism: A Coloring Book for Peers and Siblings.* Future Horizons; 1st edition, 2003.

Bleach, Fiona. *Everybody Is Different: A Book for Young People Who Have Brothers or Sisters with Autism.* Autism Asperger Publishing Company, 2002.

Coyne, Phyllis, Nyberg, Colleen, and Vendenburg, Mary Lou. *Developing Leisure Time Skills for Persons with Autism: Structured Playtime Activities with Valuable Support Strategies for Adults.* Future Horizons, 2011.

DeRoches Rosa, Shannon, and Byde Myers, Jennifer, Ditz, Liz, and 2 others. *Thinking Person's Guide to Autism.* Edited by Shannon Des Roches Rosa, Jennifer Byde Myers, Liz Ditz, Emily Willingham and Carol Greenburg. Fifty-five essays written by contributors from the autism community in all walks of life. Deadwood City Publishing, 2011.

Fowler, Melanie and Seth. *Look at My Eyes: Autism Spectrum Disorders: Autism and PDD-NOS.* Brown Books Publishing Group, 2011.

Grandin, Temple. *Thinking in Pictures, Expanded Edition: My Life with Autism.* Vintage, 2006.

Grandin, Temple, PhD. *The Way I See It, Revised and Expanded 2nd Edition: A Personal Look at Autism and Asperger's.* Future Horizons; 2nd edition, 2011.

Keating-Velasco, Joanna L. *A Is for Autism, F Is for Friend: A Kid's Book for Making Friends with a Child Who Has Autism.* Autism Asperger Publishing Company; 1st edition, 2007.

LaBosh, Kathy, and Miller, LaNita. *The Child with Autism at Home & in the Community: Over 600 Must-Have Tips for Making Home Life and Outings Easier for Everyone.* Future Horizons, 2011.

Miller, Suzy. *AWESOMISM!: A New Way to Understand the Diagnosis of Autism.* iUniverse, 2008.

Notbohm, Ellen. *Ten Things Every Child with Autism Wishes You Knew.* Future Horizons; 2nd edition, 2012.

Sabin, Ellen. *The Autism Acceptance Book: Being a Friend to Someone with Autism.* Watering Can Press; 1st edition, 2006.

Sheahan, Bobbi, and DeOrnellas, Kathe, PhD. *What I Wish I'd Known about Raising a Child with Autism: A Mom and a Psychologist Offer Heartfelt Guidance for the First Five Years.* Deadwood City Publishing, 2011.

Shore, Stephen, Rastelli, Linda G., and Grandin, Temple. *Understanding Autism for Dummies.* For Dummies; 1st edition, 2006.

Stillman, William. *The Soul of Autism: Looking Beyond Labels to Unveil Spiritual Secrets of the Heart.* Savants Paperback Career Press, 2008.

Walter, Sharie. *Crazy Love: A Traumedy about Life with Autism.* CreateSpace Independent Publishing Platform, 2011.

Zysk, Veronica. *1001 Great Ideas for Teaching and Raising Children with Autism Spectrum Disorders.* Future Horizons; 1st edition, 2004. (Winner of the 2006 Teachers' Choice Award)

Zysk, Veronica, and Notbohm, Ellen. *1001 Great Ideas for Teaching and Raising Children with Autism or Asperger's,* Revised and Expanded 2nd Edition. Future Horizons, 2010.

Vaccine Books

Coulter, Harris. *Vaccination, Social Violence, and Criminality: The Medical Assault on the American Brain.* North Atlantic Books; 1st edition, 1993.

Diodati, Catherine J.M. *Immunization: History, Ethics, Law and Health.* Integral Aspects Inc, 1999.

Hume, Ethel. *Pasteur Exposed.* The C.W. Daniel Company Ltd; 2nd edition, 1988.

Kirby, David. *Evidence of Harm: Mercury in Vaccines and the Autism Epidemic: A Medical Controversy.* St. Martin's Press; 1st edition, 2005.

Koren, Tedd. *Childhood Vaccination: Questions All Parents Should Ask.* Koren Publications, Inc., 2000.

Lydall, Wendy. *Raising a Vaccine Free Child.* AuthorHouse, 2005.

Mendelso, Robert S. *How to Raise a Healthy Child in Spite of Your Doctor*. Ballantine Books, 1987.

Miller, Neil Z. *Vaccines: Are They Really Safe and Effective?* New Atlantean Press; revised updated edition, 2011.

Miller, Neil Z. *Vaccines, Autism and Childhood Disorders: Crucial Data That Could Save Your Child's Life*. New Atlantean Press, 2010.

Murphy, Jamie. *Vaccination, Social Violence, and Criminality: The Medical Assault on the American Brain*. Earth Healing Products; 1st edition, 1993.

Murphy, Jamie. *What Every Parent Should Know about Childhood Immunization*. Earth Healing Products; 1st edition, 1993.

O'Shea, David. *The Sanctity of Human Blood: Vaccination Is Not Immunization*. NewWest; 5th edition, 2001.

Scheibner, Ivera. *Vaccination: 100 Years of Orthodox Research*. Co-Creative Designs, 1993.

Tenpenny, Sherri. *Vaccines: The Risks, the Benefits, the Choices, a Resource Guide for Parents*. Insight Publishing; 1st edition, 2006. Also available as a DVD.

Walene, James. *Immunization: The Reality Behind the Myth*. Second Edition, Revised and Updated. Praeger; 2nd edition, 1995.

Children of Now Websites

Dr. Meg's sites

Main: *www.spiritlite.com*

Touching the Light: *www.touchingthelight.org*

Dr. Meg's Specific Child-related Pages

Is your child a Crystalline Child? *www.spiritlite.com/child_crystalline.php*

Is your child a Child of the Stars? *www.spiritlite.com/child_stars.php*

Bullying and suicide information and help avenues: *www.suicide.org/bullying-and-suicide-information.html*

PMH Atwater's Websites

Main: *http://pmhatwater.hypermart.net*

A general information site with links to others: *www.metagifted.org/topics/metagifted/indigo/*

Inspired Parenting: *www.inspiredparentingmagazine.com/articles/articles.html*

Autism and Asperger's Websites

Suzy Miller's Websites

www.suzymiller.com

www.naturaltreatmentforautism.com (with Bill Tiller)

General Websites

Adventures in Autism: *http://adventuresinautism.blogspot.com/*

Age of Autism: *www.ageofautism.com/*

Anne Dachel: *www.annedachel.com/*

Asperger's Disorder Homepage: *www.aspergers.com/*

Asperger Syndrome | What is Autism? | Autism Speaks: *www.autismspeaks.org/what-autism/asperger-syndrome*

Asperger's Test Site: *info@aspergerstestsite.com*

Autism Aid: *www.autismaid.org/*

The Autism File: *www.autismfile.com/*

Autism is Medical: *www.meetup.com/Autism-Is-Medical/*

Autism One: *www.autismone.org/*

Autism Research Institute: *www.autism.com/*

The Bolen Report: *www.bolenreport.com/*

The Canary Party: *www.canaryparty.org/*

Elizabeth Birt Center for Autism Law & Advocacy: *www.ebcala.org/*

Gaia Health: *www.gaia-health.com/*

Generation Rescue: *www.generationrescue.org/*

Linderman Unleashed: *http://radio.naturalnews.com/Archive-LindermanUnleashed.asp*

The Misuta Project: *www.youtube.com/user/ljactivist*

National Autism Association: *http://nationalautismassociation.org/*

National Vaccine Information Center: *www.nvic.org/*

Natural News Radio: *http://radio.naturalnews.com/*

The Puzzling Piece: *www.thepuzzlingpiece.com/*

The Refusers: *http://therefusers.com/*

Regarding Caroline: *http://regardingcaroline.com/*

Safeminds: *www.safeminds.org/*

The Sears Family: *http://askdrsears.com*

Surfers for Autism: *www.surfersforautism.org/*

Surfers Healing: *www.surfershealing.org/*

Talk About Curing Autism: *www.tacanow.org/*

The Thinking Mom's Revolution: *http://thinkingmomsrevolution.com/how-i-gave-my-son-autism/*

Vactruth: *http://vactruth.com/*

Vaxtruth: *http://vaxtruth.org/*

Vaccine Websites

National Vaccine Information Center: *http://nvic.org/*

Studies Cited

A study published in the journal *Annals of Epidemiology* (*http://www.ncbi.nlm.nih.gov/pubmed/11895129*)

A study published in the *Journal of Inorganic Biochemistry* (*http://omsj.org/reports/tomljenovic%202011.pdf*)

A study published in the *Journal of Toxicology and Environmental Health, Part A: Current Issues* (*http://www.ncbi.nlm.nih.gov/pubmed/21623535*)

A study published in the *Journal of Toxicology* (*http://www.hindawi.com/journals/jt/2013/801517/*)

A study published in the *Journal of Biomedical Sciences* (*http://www.ncbi.nlm.nih.gov/pubmed/12145534*)

A study published in the *American Journal of Clinical Nutrition* (*http://ajcn.nutrition.org/content/80/6/1611.full*)

A study published by the Department of Pharmaceutical Sciences (*http://www.ncbi.nlm.nih.gov/pubmed/14745455*)

A study published in the *Journal of Child Neurology* (*http://jcn.sagepub.com/content/22/11/1308.abstract*)

A study published in the *Journal of Child Neurology* (*http://jcn.sagepub.com/content/21/2/170.abstract*)

A study conducted by Massachusetts General Hospital (*http://www.ncbi.nlm.nih.gov/pubmed/16151044*)

A study conducted by the Department of Pediatrics at the University of Arkansas (*http://www.ncbi.nlm.nih.gov/pubmed/15527868*)

A study published in the *Public Library of Science (PLOS)* (*http://www.plosone.org/article/info%3Adoi%2F10.1371%2Fjournal.pone.0068444*)

A study conducted by the University of Texas Health Science Centre (*http://www.ncbi.nlm.nih.gov/pubmed/16338635*)

A study published in the *International Journal of Toxicology* (*http://www.ncbi.nlm.nih.gov/pubmed/12933322*)

A study published in the *Journal of Toxicology and Environmental Health* (*http://www.ncbi.nlm.nih.gov/pubmed/17454560*)

A study published by the US National Library of Medicine (*http://civileats.com/wp-content/uploads/2009/01/palmer2008.pdf*)

A study conducted by the Department of Obstetrics and Gynecology (*http://www.ane.pl/pdf/7020.pdf*)

A study conducted by The George Washington University School of Public Health (*http://www.ncbi.nlm.nih.gov/pubmed/18482737*)

A study published in the Journal Cell Biology and Toxicology (*http://www.ncbi.nlm.nih.gov/pubmed/19357975*)

A study published by the *Journal Lab Medicine* (*http://labmed.ascpjournals.org/content/33/9/708.full.pdf*)

A study published in the Journal *Neurochemical Research* (*http://www.ncbi.nlm.nih.gov/pmc/articles/PMC3264864/?tool=pubmed*)

About Meg Blackburn Losey, PhD

 **Meg Blackburn Losey, PhD**, is the author of the international bestseller *The Children of Now*. She is also the author of *Parenting the Children of Now, The Secret History of Consciousness, Touching the Light*, and, a contributor to the bestselling *The Mystery of 2012 Anthology*. She is the creator/channeler of The Living Light Cards. Dr. Meg is a Master Healer, speaker, and teacher. She is an ordained minister in both Spiritual Science and Metaphysics. She is a PhD of Holistic Life Coaching and holds a Doctoral Degree in Metaphysics.

Losey has a passion for understanding and studying consciousness. She loves to explore the ancients, sacred sites, and healing and is the foremost expert on the evolution of consciousness in children of today and the last few decades as they become adults. She has excelled in the field of Metaphysics and as an author since 1998. In addition to her 8 books she has published 7 Audio CDs in the Touching the Light series in conjunction with Grammy Award–Winning music producer Barry Goldstein.

She is the creator of the Touching the Light Healing Modality and offers year-long certification courses. Information is available at *http://touchingthelight.org*. Author website: *www.spiritlite.com*.

To Our Readers

Weiser Books, an imprint of Red Wheel/Weiser, publishes books across the entire spectrum of occult, esoteric, speculative, and New Age subjects. Our mission is to publish quality books that will make a difference in people's lives without advocating any one particular path or field of study. We value the integrity, originality, and depth of knowledge of our authors.

Our readers are our most important resource, and we appreciate your input, suggestions, and ideas about what you would like to see published.

Visit our website at *www.redwheelweiser.com* to learn about our upcoming books and free downloads, and be sure to go to *www.redwheelweiser.com/newsletter* to sign up for newsletters and exclusive offers.

You can also contact us at *info@rwwbooks.com* or at
Red Wheel/Weiser, LLC
665 Third Street, Suite 400
San Francisco, CA 94107